Cinema Derrida: The Law of Inspection in the Age of Global Spectral Media

"Through the lens of Derrida's concept of spectrality—alongside hauntology, teletechnology, and the trace—*Cinema Derrida* fills a crucial gap in contemporary scholarship by focusing on Derrida's collaborations with filmmakers and other visual artists. Stewart's close examination of the formal elements of these films and other media texts in relation to images of bodily presence demonstrates how spectrality serves as a means for the past to place the viewer in a position of continuous and endless mourning, with all of the ethical implications vis-à-vis the other that such mourning entails. Part media biography, part theoretical intervention, this book offers an original and generative entry point into thinking about images through Derrida and Derrida through images."

—Jaimie Baron, University of Alberta

"*Cinema Derrida* inhabits Derrida's corpus as a precise formal registry of techniques, specific films, and their effects and interprets the phenomenal cinematic expressiveness central to some of Derrida's most urgent critiques: community, archive, law, ethics, mourning, grief. Tracking Derrida's theory of writing to a holistic media phenomenology, Stewart organically establishes Derrida's hauntingly 'absent' film theory as an analytic grammar and an ethical cinematics. The habit of applying Derrida to cultural analysis as diagnostic prosthesis—an 'absolute habitat', after Derrida's monolingual phenomenology—becomes a confident film theory where we have sensed a 'subterranean' presence (following Peter Brunette's coining) only to reiterate its lack. Stewart's brilliant articulation of the inarticulate puts him immediately in communion with his clearest spiritual precursor, Akira Mizuta Lippit's work on Derridean cinema. *Cinema Derrida* is of unrivaled necessity. Stewart convincingly proposes that the cinematic could not possibly proceed without a sincere reckoning with Jacques Derrida like his."

—Ted Geier, University of California, Davis

Cinema Derrida

This book is part of the Peter Lang Media and Communication list.
Every volume is peer reviewed and meets
the highest quality standards for content and production.

PETER LANG
New York • Bern • Berlin
Brussels • Vienna • Oxford • Warsaw

Tyson Stewart

Cinema Derrida

The Law of Inspection in the Age of Global Spectral Media

PETER LANG

New York • Bern • Berlin
Brussels • Vienna • Oxford • Warsaw

Library of Congress Cataloging-in-Publication Data

Names: Stewart, Tyson, author.
Title: Cinema Derrida: the law of inspection in the age of global spectral
media / Tyson Stewart.
Description: New York: Peter Lang, 2020.
Based on the author's dissertation (doctoral)—Laurentian University, 2016.
Includes bibliographical references and index.
Identifiers: LCCN 2020013099 (print) | LCCN 2020013100 (ebook)
ISBN 978-1-4331-7947-1 (hardback) | ISBN 978-1-4331-8003-3 (ebook pdf)
ISBN 978-1-4331-8004-0 (epub) | ISBN 978-1-4331-8005-7 (mobi)
Subjects: LCSH: Derrida, Jacques. | Motion pictures. | Communication.
Classification: LCC B2430.D484 S745 2020 (print) | LCC B2430.D484 (ebook) |
DDC 791.43/651—dc23
LC record available at https://lccn.loc.gov/2020013099
LC ebook record available at https://lccn.loc.gov/2020013100
DOI 10.3726/b16827

Bibliographic information published by **Die Deutsche Nationalbibliothek.**
Die Deutsche Nationalbibliothek lists this publication in the "Deutsche
Nationalbibliografie"; detailed bibliographic data are available
on the Internet at http://dnb.d-nb.de/.

Still images from the film Derrida (2002) are reproduced on the cover and in the interior with
the permission of Amy Ziering, Jane Doe Films.

Table of Contents

Acknowledgements

I am grateful to the following friends who made my time working on this book both a rich and memorable experience: Martin Boucher, Stephen Broomer, Carol Chartrand, Corinne Hart, David Lacoursière, Sharla and Stan Peltier, Damien and Sorina Van Vroenhoven. Thank you to Murray McArthur, Ginette Michaud, Laurence Simmons, and Howard Wiseman for their generous and thought-provoking feedback. Michael Naas and Kas Saghafi graciously answered my questions about Derrida's thinking on the image. *Miigwech* for your enthusiasm about this project when it was in its early stages.

Alain Beaulieu fostered many of my ideas and arguments that can be found in this book. With his guidance, I was able to see the bigger picture of Derrida and deconstruction in the history of philosophy. Alain always helped me formulate better questions and encouraged me to make longer-lasting connections between ideas. *Merci*, Alain, for making the time. Thanks are equally due to Brett Buchanan for his expertise and attention to detail. Brett's support allowed me to reach beyond the strict confines of disciplinary thought. I also wish to wholeheartedly thank Hoi Cheu for the long, frank discussions we've had on filmmaking, (anti-)philosophy, university politics, and life in general. As a virtuoso teacher, Hoi has inspired many students to reach their potential. His commitment to film and literary studies education will no doubt give me hope in times to come.

An alternate version of chapter five entitled "Before the Law of Spectrality: Derrida on the Prague Imprisonment" was published in *Empedocles: European Journal for the Philosophy of Communication* in 2018. I would like to thank the editors of that journal, especially Johan Siebers and Carlos Roos, for their careful readings. This book would not have been possible without the support I received at the Derrida Today conferences in 2016 and 2018. Thank you to the conference organizers, especially Nicole Anderson.

Four libraries or archives were key to the development and finalization of this project. They are the J.N. Desmarais Library at Laurentian University, the Toronto Reference Library, York University's Clara Thomas Archives and Special Collections, and l'Institut Mémoires de l'édition contemporaine in Basse-Normandie, France. I would like to thank the highly skilled staff at l'IMEC in particular who kept finding documents directly pertaining to my project throughout my stay there in 2015.

I would like to thank my editor at Peter Lang, Erika Hendrix, whose clear and timely feedback made the process of publishing this work remarkably pleasant.

I am most grateful to my family for their unceasing love and support. *Miigwech* to my mom, Debbie, for taking me to France when I was young and always supporting my passions. My grandmother Audrey helped with the French translations—I am forever in her debt. Thanks to my grandfather Gerry and my aunt Kelly for giving me direction. To my other grandparents, Marjorie and Eddie, *miigwech* for your hospitality and love when I needed it.

Megan, my partner and best friend, has brought so much joy to my life. She has inspired and invigorated me in every way possible. *Tu es mon coeur.*

Introduction

Spectrality plays a decisive role in Derridean aesthetics, as a small but growing literature situated primarily in philosophy and film studies attests. Postmodernist critics and scholars (i.e. Fisher, Lippit, Saghafi) have found relevant concepts in Derrida's work, especially for addressing the problem of presentism and teleological thinking. "Spectrality is at work everywhere, and more than ever, in an original way, in the reproducible virtuality of photography or cinema," (*Paper Machine* 158) Derrida notes in a long interview that touches on his role in *D'ailleurs, Derrida* (dir. Fathy, France, 1999). Simon Morgan Wortham notes, "[T]he spectre in Derrida is to be thought in terms of deconstruction's thinking of non-present remainder at work in every text, entity, being or 'presence'" (197). An initial, quick definition of spectrality might describe it as a kind of inheritance that regards you, but that cannot be seen, as in *Specters of Marx*. In photography studies, the spectre is the "having-been-there" of the photographic trace, and the internalization of the other (and the other's death), as in Kas Saghafi's *Apparitions—Of Derrida's Other*. The literature on spectral cinema utilizes deconstructive modes of analysis. However, there is a lack of agreement in this body of work about the "consequences" of spectrality, what constitutes spectral strategies within cinema, the spectral effects of traditional film form, or indeed the role film plays in connecting spectrality to mourning.

With postmodernism there is a break from the past and all we are left with ostensibly is history without the foundations that would make it a teleological process. Deconstruction's critique of the transcendental signifier helped pave the way for much of this shift in thinking. *Hauntology* comes into high relief with post-modernism and post-structuralist philosophical movements to articulate the haunting of the trace. Post-structuralism is the last great philosophical attempt to explain this sense of flickering between presence and absence, and how spectrality stages an encounter with the other and with the law of another time. I draw out the main tenets of spectrality from Derrida's seminal texts *Of Grammatology* and *Specters of Marx* and other writings, like *Echographies of Television*, in order to fill a gap in studies of Derrida and film. Throughout the book, I explain how various techniques and spectral effects such as slow motion, stillness, repetition, framing and cutting, and focus on body parts/bodily presence bring about a structure of spectrality wherein the past other returns to make impressions and ethical demands on the viewer. For this project, I draw on communication, media, and film theorists, including Jaimie Baron, Barthes, Edgar Morin, Mulvey, Michael Naas, and John Durham Peters.

Traditionally, objectivity has been associated with what is observable, present, and in the light, whereas the subject is dark and invisible. When being and non-being are blurred, all social, cultural, artistic activity and all human sciences must adapt to new ways of assessing truth. Hauntology is the return of this half-presence, when the presence seems to emerge out of the absence of meaning in the supplement. When hauntology becomes the norm/noun replacing centuries of logocentric thought, a new era without solid footing begins. While hauntology designates all that blurs the distinction between being and non-being through its temporal disjunctions, spectrality is the micro phenomenon of the encounter with the revenant. If spectrality is the coming back—*revenant*—spontaneous return of something past, hauntology is the bigger umbrella under which spectres are constantly created and disseminating. If the forces of spectrality are strongest in cinema, as Derrida claimed, then cinema takes a privileged position in our era of hauntology.

For Jacques Derrida, mourning wasn't something you did every once in a while, like when your parents die. All experience, all memorization, all encounters with the other pass through the work of mourning. He writes memorably about the death of friends, like Roland Barthes, Louis Marin, Michel Foucault, Louis Althusser, and Sarah Kofman. His eulogies were assembled and published together as *The Work of Mourning* in 2001. Derrida argued the work of mourning should be a political act, to keep the other alive, to not disrespect them by going on without them either by replacing their words, denying them the chance to speak or by only using their words and therefore not properly marking their deaths and honouring them. By not fully assimilating the dead, the work of mourning delays and defers full comprehension of the dead other, thus offering justice to the dead. In her book *Precarious Life*, Judith Butler compels us to identify with grief, as mourning is an essential part of humanizing the other. Western culture has a tendency to cover the deaths of Western casualties of war, marking their deaths in obituaries and special news reports. "By insisting on a common corporeal vulnerability," she adds, "I may seem to be positing a new basis for humanism" (42). For her, death is at once necessary and intolerable. Butler urges us to imagine alternative ways of bearing witness and marking the lives of others.

After 1989 and the fall of European communist states, Derrida writes *Specters of Marx* which describes the way Marxism will haunt world politics through, among different things teletechnology, and is thus an example of the work of political mourning in action. In this book, Derrida elaborates the idea of untimeliness, the disjunction with the present that signals events that history is not finished with or those that have not happened yet and remain to come. Untimeliness as a philosophical concept has its roots in *différance* and the divided present. In his collaboration with filmmakers throughout the years, he found new people and things to mourn, almost as though no single person or thing was worthier of mourning than any other. In each instance, philosophy and psychoanalysis work together to open a scene where the past can be reinterpreted so that the future itself can be made possible.

In mourning, the other watches us in us. Mourning suggests we incorporate narcissistically the image of who or what we love. At the very moment of narcissism we let the other in to watch over us. Narcissism is generally understood as a negative term, but, as Pleshette DeArmitt shows in *The Right to Narcissism*, there is no mourning without it. It is worth noting that Derrida offers a definition of mourning that runs counter to classical psychoanalysis. Freud guarantees successful mourning that implies appropriation of the lost object or person, whereas Lacan doesn't see the importance of mourning, insisting on lack and the inaccessibility of the past (Ricciardi 23, 45). Derrida is neither modern or fully postmodern, argues Alessia Ricciardi, especially in terms of his explanation of mourning:

> [Derrida's] primary objective is to bring to light, both within the terms of psychoanalytic inquiry and of the general culture at large, the concept of midmourning as a means of continually renegotiating or rephrasing the question of loss, and hence as a means of combatting its reification as absence … Derrida's thought ought to be understood as a synthesis of nostalgia and sublime. (34)

Mid-mourning offers "[A] domain of remembrance in which the subject is perpetually reexposed to history rather than removed from it," (34) explains Ricciardi.

The importance of mourning and keeping within the scene of mourning helps Derrida resolve—in *Specters of Marx* and elsewhere—a number of urgent political and ethical demands made clear by modern society's reluctance to learn from the past perhaps best exemplified in the speedy rhythms of communication and consumerism that flat-out deny history. If spectrality is the structure of an oscillation between the past and present, absence and presence, death and life, the virtual and the actual, with a focus on the future, then its form perfectly parallels *mid*-mourning.

Film and photography provide the structure of spectrality, a suspense opened by the missing referent. Film is of the visible, of the other that comes before, and thus of inheritance and mourning. In a sense, film and photography allows a deconstruction of the present to perpetually transform our subjectivities and by offering us half-present body parts, film also creates new kinds of archive fever. But unlike the mourning of a friend or even someone we might know tangentially, with telecommunication technology we are propelled to mourn the other, someone we really don't know and have never been close to. That's why spectrality has to do with the Levinasian other. There is an element of shock and violence that occurs with spectrality that necessarily has to be there. Yet, we interiorize the other but without totally appropriating the other. The other must retain its infinite otherness because we simply can't claim to have totally understood him. Without this successful failure, there would simply be no democracy to come.

Cinema is often called the art of illusion. Motion is only simulated, as are many of its other effects. The spectrality effect is a highly complex model or structure of inevitable asymmetry, a relationship with the other that should be recognized as a powerful element of film and indeed Derrida's work in film. As a critical tool and concept, spectrality allows us to recognize the role of mourning in our experience of cinema. Furthermore, I make the argument that it is specifically through this notion that Derrida's philosophical output becomes more ethically-driven at a time when deconstruction was being criticized for its supposed lack of politics. Film studies can help us understand spectrality perhaps more than any other field: performance, apparatus theory, theories of photography, narrative and montage theory, and histories of the technology of film offer specific explanations of how this effect happens. Film studies is best suited to take up these questions and relate them back to the themes in Derrida's own work because of its broad interdisciplinary nature.

Edgar Morin deploys the concept of the double in *The Cinema, or the Imaginary Man*: "The double is much more than a fantasy from the origins of humankind. It wanders around us and imposes its presence upon our slightest relaxation, at our first terror, in our supreme fervor" (29–30). The double in Morin is another, magical self, an alter ego created by "reflections, dreams." From a Derridean perspective, one condition of spectrality is that we cannot just simply distinguish between our "real" and spectral (or virtual) selves and memories, as such it draws on the powers of the uncanny.

Morin builds on anthropology to assess the role of magic in the modern world, and he sees cinema as a pre-Enlightenment cultural form that requires the kind of belief that modern societies claim to have dissolved. Hyper-rationality and logocentrism, scientific views of the world, effectively ignore the ghostly. And they remain all the more ignorant for it. In *Cinema*, Morin develops the notion of projection-identification to explain the uncanny double produced by cinema. For him, "[i]dentification incorporates the environment into the self and integrates it affectively" (86). The other on screen is reified in the Marxist sense (97). Morin's explanation of projection-identification would seem to produce an assimilated spectre, one no longer outstripped by the other's sheer infinity. Our double isn't a something or someone that we can always accurately locate and pin down. Doppelgängers are always travelling without us. As Freud would argue, the uncanny suggests identification with the other to the point where all distance is closed (141–142). But the spectre sees my inner thoughts and yet has its *own life*; how does this communicative structure work? The other won't haunt us, won't speak to us if we don't learn to stay within mourning. This project advocates the work of mourning.

In her short essay, "Making 'Derrida'—An Impression Or: How to Make a Film About Someone Who Doesn't Want a Film Made About Them and Whose Work—To Put it Mildly—At First Glance Would Appear to Resist Any and All Cinematic Treatment," Amy Ziering lists a half dozen films that inspired her while making her first documentary film: *Notebook on Cities and Clothes* (dir. Wim Wenders, West Germany/France, 1989), *Sans soleil* (dir. Chris Marker, France, 1983), *The Player* (dir. Robert Altman, US, 1992), *The Limey* (dir. Steven Soderbergh, US, 1999), *Two or Three Things I know About Her* (dir. Jean-Luc Godard, France, 1967), *La Chinoise* (dir. Jean-Luc Godard, France, 1967), and *JLG by JLG* (dir. Jean-Luc Godard, France, 1994)—comprised of deeply self-reflexive films, frequently commenting on themselves, using montage strategies to create philosophical thought, and offering a polyphony of voices and genres, this selection may seem deceptively straightforward: Ziering, a first-time director, needed cinematic models that would help her while editing her documentary film about her former teacher, Jacques Derrida (Dick and Ziering Kofman 25). In fact, this list of films made by highly intelligent filmmakers, who knew something about continental thought, provides incredibly apt examples of cinematic integrations of deconstructive ideas. Godard's references to Derrida in the 1969 film *Le gai savoir*

(France/West Germany) and then again in 2010s *Film socialisme* (Switzerland/ France) suggest his continued relevance for the ex-New Waver. And while film-makers like Steven Soderbergh refer to the inventive editing strategies of their films as "deconstructive,"[1] there is still no sustained theorization on how filmmak-ers have put deconstruction into cinematic language, and how Derrida encouraged this integration.

One way he sought this integration was by accepting parts in various film projects from the early 1980s to the early 2000s. Derrida's collaborations and appearances in film, beginning with 1983s *Ghost Dance* (dir. Ken McMullen, West Germany/UK) and ending with 2002s biographical documentary *Derrida* (dir. Dick and Ziering, US), are unique in the history of philosophy. Derrida embraced popular art forms and media in more ways than one: not only did he start making more public appearances after years of refusing to have his photo taken in the 1960s and 1970s (Peeters 442), his philosophy started to draw more explicitly from visual culture and artistic endeavours. While I offer explanations of this transition, I don't suppose to give any definitive accounts of this stage in Derrida's life and career. In fact, I contend the image of "Jacques Derrida" that emerges from the film and TV appearances is spectral, constantly deferring a complete grasp of him.

There are roughly four points to make, four occasions of spectrality that should be differentiated. The first description of the deconstructive ghost concentrates on the photographic medium and delay. Photography theorists have stressed the kind of encounter with the other that deconstruction values, principally because of its ghostly effects. Film and photography studies have examined the medium's relation to death for many years. Derrida argues delay is a main feature of photog-raphy. Second, I discuss how *Ghost Dance* and *Zina*'s exploration of the interioriza-tion of the disembodied other captures cinema's relation to mourning in general. This part will develop a discussion of how Derrida's late work *Specters of Marx* came out of a changing notion of spectrality, from general ideology to what can be described as ethical inheritance.

The third conjuring we want to analyze is the experience of being photographed as a spectral encounter that renders one blind. The performances of Derrida in Fathy's *D'ailleurs, Derrida* and McMullen's *Ghost Dance* will demonstrate the prin-ciples of spectrality and postal logics in terms of the overwhelming sense of blind-ness that comes with the autoportrait. If the second ghost stresses the experience of watching film, the third looks at the spectre from the point of view of the Actor. The fourth conjuring draws on the first three to elaborate a notion of the archive and archive fever in terms of how the spectral works in film, how the cinematic spectre becomes a source of origin of the archive (a film's archive, a genre's archive, a discourse's archive, *any* archive). Spectral belief functions smoothly in an era of advanced teletechnology. In all instances, we speak to the ghosts produced by tele-technology. Derrida's views on how belief and cinema are tied are read against the background of cinematic realism, performance, biography, and politics.

Approximately four ghosts or themes of conjuring, each explaining and grappling with the structure of spectrality in the hauntological era, will form the backbone of a study that also examines how Derrida's work in and on film may have further philosophical and historical value, especially for film studies. It is important to describe the philosopher's interest in film and photography because in a completely unique way it shows how deconstruction was able to adapt to a medium that seems to capture the subject in a completely different way than the written word. Spectrality is about communicating with a phantom, with the fiction, the virtual. It is a structure based on suspense that photography makes possible. It's about the possibility of an origin that remains nevertheless tied to the borderlines of the image. As such, it is meant to be critique and explication, warning and elucidation.

In Chapter One, "The Blinding Promises of Spectrality: Derrida's Communication Theory," I draw on communication theory to move from a general understanding of haunted media and Spirit to the inner workings of the spectre as spelled out by Derrida. Beyond Freud's uncanny, spectrality gathers the powers of mourning, blindness, inheritance, and Law. In *Specters of Marx*, Derrida stresses the out of joint, temporal dimension of spectrality. The fact that the spectre speaks to us from another time that is now out of joint with the world reality relates spec-trality to justice. Moreover, as spectrality moves from a general concept of haunting to an encounter with the other, it requires an ethical response and responsibility. I summarize the tenets of deconstruction as a form of archi-writing and argue the importance of blindness in deconstructing the visible. As soon as there is spec-tral structure or the promise of presence, blindness comes in to challenge every instance of self-presence in visibility. Derrida makes blindness a key element of spectrality in *Specters of Marx*, *Echographies of Television*, *Memoirs of the Blind*, and other texts.

Chapter Two ("1st *Séance*: Photography's Suspense Effect") explores how delay functions in cinema in relation to the suspense effect that is constitutive of both *différance* and photography. After an examination of the role of the photographic in deconstruction through later texts by Derrida and in secondary literature (i.e. Naas and Saghafi), I relate deconstruction to apparatus film theories by Braudy and Mulvey and highlight the importance of Derrida's thought for apparatus the-ory more broadly. Throughout this section, I question the assumption that the distinguishing feature of cinema, and the one that gives it its claims to realism, is motion. The use of slow motion in *La jetée* (dir. Marker, France, 1962), Godard's

Every Man for Himself (France, 1980), and, finally, *Derrida* can be described as deconstructive in this regard.

The third chapter and second *séance* "2ⁿᵈ *Séance*: The Dead Sound Off: Mourning Others in *Ghost Dance*" demonstrates how *Specters of Marx*'s "cinematic" argument is in dialogue with Ken McMullen's mournful films *Ghost Dance* and *Zina*. Pascale Ogier, who plays the protagonist in *Ghost Dance*, died at the age of 25, a couple of years after the release of the film. On his long scene in which he improvises an answer to her question, "Do you believe in ghosts?" Derrida says in a 1992 interview, exactly one year before the publication of *Specters of Marx*,

> In my response I presented some variations on the theme of spectrality that, far from being reduced by the rationality of modern technology, found itself, on the contrary, amplified, as if this medium (photocinematography, teleperception, teleproduction, telecommunication) was the very site, the proper element (also properly privileged), of a fantastical phantomaticity, of the *phainesthai* in its originary link with *technê*. The revenant is not confined to the culture of the manor house or to the spiritualism and fantastic literature from the last century. Every culture has its phantoms and the spectrality that is conditioned by its technology. (*Copy* 39)

I want to stress this link between apparition—*phainesthai*—ghost and the machine, technology, and media, because this film is unique in the way it explores these connections, not only because it contains Derrida's first elaboration of the theory of spectrality. While *Ghost Dance* investigates the role of mourning and political inheritance in terms of media and communication technologies, *Zina* does the same but contains an explicit generational drama in the form of Trotsky and his daughter, both exiled characters that haunt each other. *Ghost Dance* and *Zina*'s experimentations with sound and image and other formal innovations are important for the elaboration of the structure of spectrality and its related consequences (Law, mourning, alterity) in *Specters* and other related texts that he writes in this period.

Chapter Four ("3ʳᵈ *Séance*: Before the Law of Spectrality: Derrida on the Prague Imprisonment") charts Derrida's performances in front of the camera and argues several different film retellings of his 1982 imprisonment in Prague articulate the connections between spectrality and Law. If spectrality disrupts the binary of presence and absence, then we must not only show how there is presence within the context of film viewing, but also how being photographed is a matter of embracing absence. The Prague imprisonment was an intriguing event in Derrida's life because he immediately wrote about the experience. He briefly describes the fact that guards made references to Kafka during his imprisonment in the essay "Before the Law" written that same year and, in *Ghost Dance*, he reveals that he himself was researching *The Trial* at the very moment of his arrest. The incident seemed to go hand-in-hand with revoking his self-imposed ban on his public image, beginning with his first television interview on Antenne 2.

Why does Derrida replay this scene, re-enact it, indefinitely? How does the recurring trope of blindness in his writings relate to both the imprisonment and the experience of being photographed? The film retellings in *Ghost Dance*, *D'ailleurs, Derrida*, and, finally, *Derrida* could be a way of changing the ghosts that haunt that scene: from anguish in the first television version to openness toward the other in *D'ailleurs, Derrida*, where the place and time of the event are not named. By the time we get to *D'ailleurs, Derrida*, it is as if the author of the event was alterity itself. Through a comparison with other French philosophers in the media at the time, such as Foucault and Deleuze, I demonstrate Derrida's unique approach to film and photography as both blinding and mournful forms of hauntology.

In the final chapter, "4th *Séance*: Cinécircumcision: Phantom Parts in the Archive," I offer an analysis of the archival effect in documentary film and its (often ironic) quest for presence. The presence of body and the role of the eyeline and gaze (the cinematic equivalents of retracing the other's steps) are analyzed in *Sans soleil* (dir. Marker, France, 1983), *Grizzly Man* (dir. Herzog, US, 2005) and Derrida's various documentary films. Drawing on Jaimie Baron's recent work on post-structuralist tendencies in contemporary documentary, I analyze the role of disparity and bodily proximity in Derrida's biographies. *Derrida* has been called an example of "blind cinema" by Nicholas Royle (Dick and Ziering Kofman) because its treatment of deconstruction goes beyond the visible and finds fertile ground in more tactile forms of the ghostly body. The theme of the body is explored throughout in relation to archive theory. This chapter also contains an extended analysis on the metaphor of circumcision and how Derrida himself deployed the term in reference to his own image. Finally, I suggest how the notion of the exappropriable cinematic body paves new ground for Derridean interpretations of film.

In the documentary biographies, Fathy, Ziering, and Dick bring Derrida's image into play and make powerful contributions to his life's work. Even though in *D'ailleurs, Derrida* we see images of Algeria and words of his childhood from *Circonfession*, the film seems to explicitly challenge the notion of an origin of Derrida (his biography, so his life, his image, his philosophy). Derrida argues as much in *Tourner les mots* when he describes the ghostliness of performing in front of the camera and the issue of the postal, addressing the unknown, quite literally sending pieces of himself to unknown places, addressing unknown "spectators," performing for the ghost, as a ghost, looking at himself, becoming-ghost, addressing no *one*. As the films integrate deconstructive principles into their structure, they are also portraits of the man himself in image and in sound, responding to the demands of the conventions of documentary.

This book could have followed a number of paths. Social science approaches like Lamont's 1987 essay on the celebrity and influence of Derrida in academia are important for grounding deconstruction as a cultural good in a material sociocultural context. What was the relation between the film productions and Derrida's own philosophical trajectory? The semi-biographical approach that I've taken allows for a deeper investigation of Derrida's philosophical path. *Ghost Dance* allows Derrida to offer an explanation of the ghostly nature of cinema in a film that examines ghosts from mostly postmodern and post-structuralist perspectives. His work on TV, especially the interview with Adler clearly saw him improvising on the technical experience of live television. Then there is the major curatorial and philosophical event that is *Memoirs of the Blind*. And Derrida's quest to expand the margins of philosophy reaches a climax with two feature-length (auto)biographical documentaries that treat his late ideas with the utmost philosophical care.

In film theory, older approaches like Marxist ideology critique or psychoanalytic critiques of the male gaze have dominated the field and especially its instruction, but they don't even approach the role of mourning and spectrality. Other approaches tend to study narrative and stylistic elements that signify one thing or another. My study is a counter-intuitive film theory that Derrida began to develop, mostly in relation to his own collaborations with filmmakers from the 1980s onwards, and therefore mostly in the later part of his career and philosophical output. Derrida's work on spectrality traverses both film and text. That is why my study can also be described as a media biography; I conducted research on his life and work in his archive at L'Institut Mémoires de l'édition contemporaine in Basse-Normandie, France, and often the borders between the work and life aren't rigorously drawn. His collaborations with filmmakers allowed deconstruction to evolve in exciting ways. I analyze this integration through close textual analysis of both the writings and films. By looking at media and mourning in 1983s *Ghost Dance*, blindness in 1999s *D'ailleurs, Derrida*, and phantasmatic presence, delay, and the counter-signature in 2002s *Derrida*, along with various photographs and television appearances throughout the years, my study argues that these collaborations allowed Derrida to expand the parameters of deconstruction from a literary and textual theory to one that included film and photography, which turn out of have a significant ethical dimension that is understood very little.

Cinema Derrida looks at Derrida's collaborations in visual media and his appearances in primarily visual arts, television, photography, and film. These media artefacts helped shape perceptions of Derrida in France and in US. Derrida used media as a supplemental form of philosophical discourse that allowed him to simultaneously carve out a public image and provide traditional philosophy something it did not have, textually, rhetorically, and institutionally: philosophy became a creative enterprise under Derrida's direction. Works like *Truth in Painting*, *The Post Card*, *Glas*, and *Memoirs of the Blind* rubbed up against the very margins of philosophy. Even the television interviews, where Derrida more explicitly dons the role of reflexive media intellectual could be described as a performance. His 1996 appearance on *Cercle de minuit* flew in the face of what was conventionally done on the philosophical talk show by paying attention to the tele-technics of modern television. One way to demonstrate how Derrida challenged generic forms of communication is to look at the other public intellectuals that were in the media circuit at the time of Derrida's appearances (roughly from the early 1980s to his death in 2004). By reflexively deconstructing each medium he was using, Derrida had a more complex relation to popular discourse than other public intellectuals, especially those in France at the time, like Bourdieu, Foucault, Deleuze, and Bernard-Henri Lévy.

In recent years, Derrida's theory of hauntology has become influential in film studies. The way theorists have brought together photography-based arts, like film, and spectrality shows a continued engagement with Derridean philosophy and visual culture. Each time the concept is used in writings on the visual arts and media, the author connects spectrality to a different Derridean topic: *différance* in Burchill; blindness in Lippit; the other in Saghafi; authorship in Guthrie; temporality in Cowie. While all these studies make significant breakthroughs, they avoid describing how the notion of spectrality developed relatively slowly in Derrida's oeuvre and how Derrida's collaborations in film actually drove the development and application of the concept. What are the connections between Derrida's written texts, like *Droit de regards*, *Specters of Marx*, and *Echographies of Television*, and his work with filmmakers and visual artists? This aspect of Derrida's archive still needs to be developed and explored.

While staying near Derrida's writings on spectrality, my contribution in particular will be to highlight the relation between spectrality and established concepts in film studies, like reflexivity, performance, and montage. An unfinished task of Derridean thought seeks to make the visual arts an object of philosophical inquiry, and the advantages of seeing cinema as a form of spectrality include complicating the notion of authorship and making cinema the scene of visual mourning. In *Echographies of Television*, Derrida explains how spectrality is a matter of rights. In what follows I trace the concept of spectrality from its earliest iterations in *Droit de regards* to "Le cinéma et ses fantômes." The goal is to clarify, work on, work with, and expand the notion while also pointing out just how it relates to film and where it gets expressed through the medium's temporal and technical qualities.

One area of film studies that would seem most apt for a deconstructive analysis is film-philosophy, a relatively small subfield of film studies that tends to reproduce conceptual and metaphysical categories either in its continental or analytical and empirical forms (Trifonova). Roger Scruton and Dominic Mciver Lopes in Carroll and Choi's *Philosophy of Film and Motion Pictures* have theorized photography as pure transparency. Jacques Rancière has also put forward the view that photographic images are self-evident views of the world. To understand the image, these theorists argue, we no longer require special training or knowledge or *even* belief. These kinds of works imply metaphysical concepts of the image and often pursue a logocentric view of realism, a move importantly undertaken by André Bazin. Documentary film professes to unfold in a linear way in the present-tense. Trifonova sees the recent rejection of critical theory as nothing more than an encroaching neoconservatism, adding, "[M]erely increasing the number of historical or material facts to be studied does not automatically increase the amount of theoretical knowledge these facts can offer us, or their political usefulness" (xxiii). These mostly analytic and cognitivist perspectives claim that humans watch films very much in the same way: "[E]ven as they criticize the essentialism and idealism of Continental theory cognitivists, too, put forward an ontological claim, although one about the human mind rather than about cinema or reality" (Trifonova xxiv).

In contemporary continental philosophy, Derrida had the uncanny ability to speak to ghosts. Unlike Freud, Marx, analytic philosophy, and Western science, Derrida *spoke* to ghosts. This book posits that one significant way in which Derrida conjured the ghost and made way for spectrality was through cinema. The medium's iterabilty and its death effect allowed Derrida to adapt spectrality and deconstruction to filmmaking in a broad sense. Much media studies tends to seek out authenticity in its materialist form and stresses the turn away from content as if this would ensure more certainty (Kittler; Parikka). The irretrievable loss that comes with the digital justifies media studies' dismissal of content. What they are responding to is loss in general and so they choose the more empirical approach of dealing with real, material objects. The power of spectrality increases in the new media, digital age. As we get further away from the authentic truth, the desire to return gets stronger. The desire to desire something that has been lost and will no doubt stay lost is the full structure of spectrality. Is spectrality different in different media contexts? Jeffrey Sconce calls it "electronic presence" in his study that looks at accounts of mystic moments in the history of telegraphy, TV, film, radio, and computers but fails to explore the full phenomenon of spectrality. My goal is to develop the notion of spectrality in Derrida's collaboration in film in terms that are amenable to deconstruction, for I believe Derrida himself understood the importance of spectrality in relation to film studies. Even as new research seeks to develop spectrality in relation to film (Jeong and Andrew; Saghafi; Blanco and Peeren), it is still after all a little understood term in the field.

An early book-length study of Derrida and film theory, *Screen/Play*, spells out a number of post-structuralist critiques of film studies and ways of potentially undertaking a deconstructive approach to filmmaking. Auteurism and Lacanian psychoanalysis were still highly influential to film studies when Brunette and Wills brought deconstruction to bear on the field. One of the questions the book asks is if speech has been privileged over writing, the basis of *Of Grammatology*, what is the cinematic corollary? The image over sound? Or realism over montage? Bazin argues that the long take and long deep focus shot transparently captures the richness of reality (*What Is Cinema?*). This informs how documentary is conceptualized as a genre of visual evidence. Elsewhere, Robert Smith's notable essay on deconstruction and cinema draws on "To Speculate—on 'Freud'" to show how *Jurassic Park*'s (dir. Spielberg, US, 1993) diegetic elements, such as the character of the park's owner and the park apparel, have direct corollaries in the real world, thus putting the film's exclusively fictional aspects into question, like Derrida did with Freud's "science." But there is little difference between Smith's approach here and other mainstream postmodernist views (Nichols; Baudrillard). Film studies on the whole has become an interdisciplinary field with methodologies coming from semiotics, history, labour, women's studies, etc. The field today is comprised of a multiplicity of fields. Yet Derrida's absence in film studies is notable, especially because thinkers like Lacan have been so incredibly influential (Brunette and Wills, *Screen/Play* 16).

One way in which Derrida and this book break with textual criticism in film studies is by looking at film as a process. We reject the notion that film studies should be limited to structuralist accounts of auteur filmmakers or discovering masterpieces. What will become clear is the broadness of scope of this study that deconstruction seems to encourage. As Brunette and Wills note,

> Once the critique turns to the wider context of the apparatus of cinema, any remaining hint of ideas of directness and immediacy, such as obtain in the image-reference relation, is dispelled by the complex system of production and reception ... The complicity between textual operations and the operations of the viewing experience that feminist psychoanalytic theorists have delineated, the so-called complicity of the looks comprising cinema and their repetition through various mechanisms of the apparatus, as well as the unique type of mirror that the screen comes to represent in such discussions—all these matters can be read as pointing to the structure of differential repetition that underwrites cinema as writing. (*Screen/Play* 76–77)

Surprisingly, when asked about the role of discourse in cinema, Derrida said, "[T]he most effective deconstruction, and I have said this often, is one that deals with the nondiscursive, or with discursive institutions that don't have the form of a written discourse" (Brunette and Wills, *Deconstruction* 14). As Derrida claims in an interview on the visual (or spatial) arts,

> [T]he general question of the spatial arts is given prominence, for it is within a certain experience of spacing, of space, that resistance to philosophical authority can be produced. In other words, resistance to logocentrism has a better chance of appearing in these kinds of art. (Brunette and Wills, *Deconstruction* 10)

Even if there is more resistance to logocentrism in film, as Derrida claims, its spatial dimension still means there is a frame including certain things and excluding others. Derrida says,

> [E]ven if there is no discourse, the effect of spacing already implies a textualization ... I would say that the idea that deconstruction should confine itself to the analysis of the discursive text—I know that the idea is widespread—is really either a gross misunderstanding or a political strategy designed to limit deconstruction to matters of language ...[T]o want to confine it to linguistic phenomena is the most suspect of operations. (Brunette and Wills, *Deconstruction* 15)

In mourning, there is always a spatial dimension as well. In order to successfully fail to mourn—the only way to mourn for Derrida—there must be a space in us that opens for the incorporation of the other, a "strange space of images and gazes" (DeArmitt, *Right to Narcissism* 120). In this geometry of gazes,

> [T]he other who is no longer, who remains wholly and infinitely other as he was in life and even more so in death, distanced in his infinite alterity, is now an image, but an image that looks at us, in us. (DeArmitt, *Right to Narcissism* 117)

The frame of the image that is outside flips around and becomes the inside within our psychic apparatus when interiorized in us, when mourned for. The inside of the image then ironically becomes the outside when interiorized within us, its subject blinding us with its Law of alterity.

It was only near the end of Derrida's career that film became the subject of his critical lens—and it was usually engaged indirectly in discussions on visual arts, television, photography, ocularcentrism. Several books on photography appeared in English later, indeed after his death, including *Athens, Still Remains* and *Copy, Archive, Signature*. Works that apply directly to film studies include *Echographies of Television*, a book that began as a television interview that never aired. Talking with Bernard Stiegler, Derrida expounds on the topics of liveness, nationalism, photography, the performance of intellectuals in the media, and spectrality, among other topics. *Tourner les mots*, another collaboration, was written with Safaa Fathy after the making of *D'ailleurs, Derrida* and released in 2000. The book is really a companion piece to the film describing its production and themes in the form of an *abécédaire*. An informative text, it deconstructs much of the film's rhetorical and documentary conventions.

In late conferences and interviews, he began addressing the topic of film and its relation to deconstruction. *Cahiers du cinéma*, that beacon of relevant film criticism in France, published a long interview with Derrida in 2001 in their 50th anniversary edition. In this interview, Derrida considers the relation between spectrality and cinema. In this piece Derrida also traces his lifelong fascination (indeed obsession) with film, starting when he was a 10 year old boy in Algeria watching French and American movies after the war to his apprenticeship film, *D'ailleurs, Derrida*. One of the problematics of studying film as spectrality is the sheer amount of ghosts that cross each other in a collective representation (79 "Le cinéma et ses fantômes"). For him, the act of viewing is also a work of mourning magnified. Derrida explains the similarities between cinema and psychoanalysis:

> Hypnosis, fascination, identification, all these terms and procedures are common to cinema and psychoanalysis, and this is the sign of "thinking together" which seems to me to be essential. Moreover, a cinema session is only a little longer than an analysis session. We go to the cinema to be analyzed, letting all of its spectres appear and speak. We can, economically (compared to an analysis session), let the spectres come back to us on the screen. (77–78 "Le cinéma et ses fantômes")[2]

At a lecture at l'Institut national de l'audiovisuel (INA) in 2002, Derrida argues that vision has been the basis of Western philosophy and thought, and makes room for the photographic arts to mount an analysis of this foundational metaphor:

> I still believe in it to some extent, we could give a thousand examples: philosophy is structured by a metaphor without metaphor of sight, precisely because of this value of presence. The *eidos*, the determination of being, in Plato, you know, means precisely the outline of a visible form. (*Penser à ne pas voir* 71)[3]

This talk was published in a collection of Derrida's writings and the interviews on the visual arts, *Penser à ne pas voir*, that appeared in 2013. In chapters like "Trace et archive, image et art," "La danse des fantômes," "Le cinéma et ses fantômes," and "Penser à ne pas voir" Derrida touches on many different elements of cinema, like the use of subtitles in international cinema, the experience of performing for the camera, and the difference between image and sound tracks. Spectrality is presented as a problematic to work through within his discussion of the privileged status of the visible.

Notes

1. Soderbergh describes *The Limey* as "deconstructive" on the DVD commentary track.
2. "[H]ypnose, fascination, identification, tous ces termes et ces procédés sont communs au cinéma et à la psychanalyse, et c'est là le signe d'un 'penser ensemble' qui me semble primordial. D'ailleurs, une séance de cinéma, ce n'est qu'un petit peu plus long qu'une séance d'analyse. On va se faire analyser au cinéma, en laissant paraître et parler tous ses spectres. On peut, de façon économe (par rapport à une séance d'analyse), laisser les spectres vous revenir sur l'écran."
3. "J'y crois toujours dans une certaine mesure, on pourrait en donner mille exemples: la philosophie est structurée par une métaphorique sans métaphore de la vue, à cause justement de cette valeur de présence. L'*eidos*, la détermination de l'être, chez Platon, comme *eidos*, vous le savez, veut dire précisément le contour d'une forme visible."

Bibliography

Baudrillard, Jean. *Simulacra and Simulation*. Trans. Sheila Glaser. Ann Arbor: University of Michigan Press, 1995.

Bazin, André. *What Is Cinema?* Trans. Hugh Gray. Berkeley: University of California Press, 1967.

Blanco, María del Pilar, and Esther Peeren, eds. *The Spectralities Reader: Ghosts and Haunting in Contemporary Cultural Theory*. London: Bloomsbury, 2013.

Brunette, Peter, and David Wills. *Screen/Play: Derrida and Film Theory*. Princeton, NJ: Princeton University Press, 1989.

———, eds. *Deconstruction and the Visual Arts: Art, Media, Architecture*. Cambridge and New York: Cambridge University Press, 1994.

Butler, Judith. *Precarious Life: The Powers of Mourning and Violence*. London: Verso, 2006.

DeArmitt, Pleshette. *The Right to Narcissism: A Case for an Im-possible Self-Love*. New York: Fordham University Press, 2014.

Derrida, Jacques. "Le cinéma et ses fantômes." Interview with Antoine de Baecque and Thierry Jousse. *Cahiers du cinéma* 556 (April 2001): 74–85.

———. *Paper Machine*. Trans. Rachel Bowlby. Stanford, CA: Stanford University Press, 2005.

———. *Copy, Archive, Signature: A Conversation On Photography*. Trans. Jeff Fort. Stanford, CA: Stanford University Press, 2010.

Dick, Kirby, and Amy Ziering Kofman, dirs. *Derrida*. 2002. DVD. Zeitgeist Video, 2003.

———, eds. *Derrida: Screenplay and Essays on the Film Derrida*. Manchester: Manchester University Press, 2005.

Freud, Sigmund. *The Uncanny*. Trans. David McLintock. London: Penguin, 2003.

Godard, Jean-Luc, dir. *Le gai savoir*. 1969. DVD. New York: Koch Lorber, 2008.

———. *Film socialisme*. 2010. DVD. New York: Kino Lorber, 2011.

Jeong, Seung-Hoon, and Dudley Andrew. "Grizzly Ghost: Herzog, Bazin and the Cinematic Animal." *Screen* 49.1 (2008): 1–12.

Kittler, Friedrich. *Gramophone, Film, Typewriter.* Trans. Geoffrey Winthrop-Young and Michael Wutz. Stanford, CA: Stanford University Press, 1999.

McMullen, Ken, dir. *Ghost Dance.* 1983. DVD. Mediabox, 2006.

Morin, Edgar. *The Cinema, or, The Imaginary Man.* Trans. Lorraine Mortimer. Minneapolis: University of Minnesota Press, 2005.

Nichols, Bill. *Blurred Boundaries: Questions of Meaning in Contemporary Culture.* Bloomington: Indiana University Press, 1994.

Parikka, Jussi. *What Is Media Archaeology?* Cambridge, UK: Polity, 2012.

Ricciardi, Alessia. *The Ends of Mourning: Psychoanalysis, Literature, Film.* Stanford, CA: Stanford University Press, 2003.

Saghafi, Kas. *Apparitions—Of Derrida's Other.* New York: Fordham University Press, 2010.

Sconce, Jeffrey. *Haunted Media: Electronic Presence from Telegraphy to Television.* Durham and London: Duke University Press, 2000.

Smith, Robert. "Deconstruction and Film." *Deconstructions: A User's Guide.* Ed. Nicholas Royle. New York: Palgrave, 2000. 119–136.

Soderbergh, Steven, dir. *The Limey.* 1999. DVD. Artisan Home Entertainment, 2000.

Trifonova, Temenuga. "Introduction: That Perpetually Obscure Object of Theory." *European Film Theory.* Ed. Temenuga Trifonova. New York and London: Routledge, 2009.

Wortham, Simon Morgan. *The Derrida Dictionary.* London and New York: Continuum, 2010.

CHAPTER ONE

The Blinding Promises of Spectrality: Derrida's Communication Theory

Of course they do not exist, so what?

—Derrida, *Specters of Marx*

This chapter describes the concept of spectrality in Derrida's writing as it relates to communication, ethics, and technology. *Specters of Marx* elaborates the significance of hauntology, the return of the repressed in metaphysical logocentrism that stresses the self-presence where the self is complete, produces action in its presence, and is in no way influenced by the dead or what isn't there. Much communication thought highlights the concept of the ghostly or spectral. From Freud to Peters, the ghostly dimension of communication is often tied to developing technology and new media and new ways of disseminating traces of the human. But Derrida's spectres aren't just scary doppelgängers or even the grounds of (mis) communication with ghosts or aliens. Spectrality has much more in its sights: *it has you in its sight with a view to put the other in you, to impregnate you with otherness.* The actual is haunted by the virtual, the living followed by the dead. That's why spectrality often has an uncomfortable relation with the form of ideology or even propaganda. Spectrality doesn't simply relate to the uncanny of Freud, but a whole constellation of issues, like mourning, blindness, inheritance, and Law. I define the temporal dimension of spectrality and the visor effect. One ushers in inheritance and justice, the other blinds you and puts you in the sights of the ghost. As spectrality moves from a general concept of haunting to one of an encounter with the other, it acknowledges the role of blindness in the visual arts and media, and how blindness allows for the very possibility of the future.

The signified has the privilege of presence. In Western structuralist thought, the sign, made up of both signifier and signified, privileges the signified because that is the content, the idea or concept. In *Of Grammatology*, Derrida claims that the transcendental signified does not have an independent, external existence. Rather, the transcendental signified is bound to the signifier. So, the signified "God," the ultimate signified, is always already tied to material writings and traces in language (13). Signs and materiality of communication are the basis of the concept. There must always be a written version of an idea. Concepts don't just exist out there, beyond our methods of communication. Derrida's critique of the transcendental signified is meant to take away the authority that comes automatically with it. This is why writing is framed as a dangerous supplement in Western philosophy. Derrida explains, "It diverts the immediate presence of thought to speech into representation and the imagination. This recourse is not only 'bizarre,' but dangerous. It is the addition of a technique, a sort of artificial and artful ruse to make speech present when it is actually absent" (*Of Grammatology* 144). Speech feigns presence because it doesn't require debasing itself by becoming material. Derrida will go to pains to show how this technique is basically how all communication happens:

> The supplement will always be the moving of the tongue or acting through the hands of others. In it everything is brought together: progress as the possibility of perversion, regression toward an evil that is not natural and that adheres to the power of substitution that permits us to absent ourselves and act by proxy, through representation, through the hands of others. Through the written. This substitution always has the form of the sign. The scandal is that the sign, the image, or the representer, become forces and make the world move. (*Of Grammatology* 147)

Bennington notes,

> All sorts of accidents can prevent my letter surviving me de facto: but de jure a letter which was not readable after my death would not be a letter. It is not necessary for me to be dead for you to be able to read me, but it is necessary for you to be able to read me even if I am dead. (Bennington and Derrida, *Jacques Derrida* 51)

Writing is not tied to an origin; it begins a phantasmic relation to the present as soon as the trace is produced. By way of example, Derrida's signature at the end of "Signature Event Context," something so personal that suggests his presence, can immediately disseminate beyond the moment of its production.

In his 1980–1981 lectures on representation, Derrida isolates representation as the nexus point, the pivot, the moment when the future is born:

According to Hegel, representation is the central moment of becoming, the pivot or the essential relay, and precisely within a structure of the already not yet ... Between the religion of revelation and philosophy as absolute knowledge, representation always marks the limit. Representation is already the next step ... It has happened that we have translated phantasia or phantasma as representation, a lexicon from Plato does it and we commonly translate the Stoic corpus this way, but it is here that the supposedly anachronistic subjectum and repraentatio are possible and thinkable for the Greeks ...[1]

The roots of hauntology in Derrida start with his deconstruction of the binary presence/non-presence and the trace in writing. The trace, which all writing depends on, marks a presence and an absence and thus problematizes the notion of a clear distinction between writing's secondary status in Western thought. *Of Grammatology* spells out many of Derrida's most important concepts, like supplementarity, writing, deconstruction, *différance*. Hauntology emerges from the presence of the trace and trace of presence that characterizes the structure of the sign in deconstruction. Spivak explains, "[T]he name of this gesture effacing the presence of a thing yet keeping it legible—is writing" (Derrida, *Of Grammatology* xli). For Derrida, writing—indeed all language—is *sous rature* (under erasure). Derrida draws on Nietzsche who advocates an active form of forgetfulness of Being. Understanding forgetfulness as both an attribute and limitation begins the deconstructive process. Forgetting in Nietzsche means rewriting. Unlike Heidegger's insistence on disclosure, Nietzsche promotes forgetting. It's the secrets that make the future possible. In Western philosophy, being is a species of logos. The voice suggests proximity and spontaneity; preconditions of "being" rely upon a privileged view of voice. But being is shot through with non-presence. As Derrida would later argue, "The being of what we are is first of all inheritance" (*Specters* 68).

Derrida's immodest project aims to show how in our new era deconstruction will prevail as an approach to studying communication and media ontology. He conceives *différance*, one could say, in order to remove the metaphysical attributes to Being and its search for fullness of meaning. *Différance* emphasizes the trace of the non-transcendental. Freud allows Derrida to think of *différance* emanating from the "self," suggesting we are a kind of free play (Derrida, *Of Grammatology* xliv). There is thus with deconstruction an imperative to be free. This is also where the democracy to come comes from. We are free, but *différance* is also related to the singular, to the other. Like a momentary (or endless) detour, *différance*, which also constitutes the subject, can only create traces of something that was never transcendent, something that was never pure and proper. The trace represents the fall, the death of the metaphysical concept:

> Since the trace is not a presence but the simulacrum of a presence that dislocates itself, displaces itself, refers itself, it properly has no site—erasure belongs to its structure. And not only the erasure which must always be able to overtake it (without which it would not be a trace but an indestructible and monumental substance), but also the erasure which constitutes it from the outset as a trace, which situates it as the change of site, and makes it disappear in its appearance, makes it emerge from itself in its production. (*Margins* 24)

But the trace is haunted by the transcendental signified and by other traces.

The system or structure of writing is perhaps Derrida's most important contribution to philosophy and critical theory. Writing in the narrow sense (letters, print) and general sense (speech, photography) slip over each other. Spivak notes, "One slips into the other, putting the distinction under erasure. Writing has had the negative privilege of being the scapegoat whose exclusion represents the definition of the metaphysical enclosure" (Derrida, *Of Grammatology* lxix). Derrida avoids making a concrete distinction between the two, so often writing starts characterizing perhaps everything we count as meaningful. Derrida is unlike most philosophers in that his transdisciplinary system of thinking avoids erecting borders around diverse phenomena. As Geoffrey Bennington puts it, "My mortality (my finitude) is thus inscribed in everything I inscribe. What is here called 'death' is the generic name we shall give to my absence in general with respect to what I write" (Bennington and Derrida 51). Writing is a ghostly business. This means within presence is absence. Technics ensures the proliferation of ghosts, and that is chiefly the topic we are interested in here.

Derrida no doubt embraced the role of technology in his own oeuvre. Of course, the first technology theorized is writing, but his interest in technology and then later teletechnologies goes back to the contamination of Being and his critique of *Dasein* in phenomenology. Bennington describes the importance of technology in Derrida's work:

> Being is nothing outside the entities in which its retrac(t)ing is marked, this thought nonetheless wants to retain a certain purity, as thought, with respect to technology. Everything we have said about possibly mechanical repetition as an essential possibility of archi-writing marks the necessity of a contamination of any essence by a generalized 'technology.' (Bennington and Derrida 312–313)

Any inscription is a form of writing, even in the visual arts. Bennington envisions a Derrida archive, acting like a supercomputer that would enable users to access his work by theme or word or page.[2] Bennington says everything Derrida referred to should also be included—

> a larger memory making accessible, according to the same multiple entries, the texts quoted or invoked by Derrida, with everything that forms their 'context,' therefore

just about the (open) totality of the universal library, to say nothing of musical or visual or other (olfactive, tactile, gustative) archives to be invented. (Bennington and Derrida 315)

Ostensibly, finding new connections in Derrida's archive would be an endless task. *Cinema Derrida* would be just one strand in such an archive.

Early writings seem to put accent on death by demonstrating how language as a form of iterability parallels death within the metaphysical tradition. The transition to spectrality is one where Derrida includes the living-dead as a new characteristic of communication in post-structuralism. Early Derrida's archi-writing acknowledges the death and iterability of the trace. Spectrality comes on the scene to show the miracle of presence within the supplementary trace. By extending Derrida's deconstruction of speech and writing, spectrality turns our attention to the living within the dead, and the dead in the liveliest speech. This now half-dead sign allows life, inheritance, Law, ethics to come in. While Derrida would never turn away from the grave consequences of absence in all language, he would nonetheless allow the politics of the other to do radical, transformative work on it. At the same time, spectrality as Law would mean power without meaning, without a name, without a history: a structure more than an argument spelling danger and total freedom.

Michael Naas explains spectrality with reference to *Speech and Phenomena*, where voice doesn't seem to need a signifier: "It thus presents itself in a way that seems to efface its signifying body, that is, its dead, mechanical body, giving access to the thing itself" (*Miracle and Machine* 145). A classic definition of self-presence posits the tension between signifier and signified is eclipsed. Naas continues,

> The fact that this effacement of the signifier or this experience of effacement is but an illusion or a phantasm does little to dampen its effect. On the contrary, its effect comes precisely from the fact that it is an illusion or phantasm. (*Miracle and Machine* 146–147)

Synchronized sound film and television, especially televangelism for Naas, caters to spectrality more than other forms of media. Naas spells it out: "Derrida's point is that certain media, chief among them television, are better able to efface themselves in order to produce such a phantasm, that is, in order to simulate a life before media and the machine" (*Miracle and Machine* 151). This is why Derrida paid close attention to sound in his *Cahiers* interview and also possibly explains why he didn't want his voice-over to be used in *Derrida*: his image and voice are purposefully sutured in his last documentary.

Psychoanalytic theory is an important bedrock for Derrida's concept of spectrality. Spectrality as such is intertwined with repression, mourning, and identity. In his essay on the uncanny, Freud makes associations between *umheimlich*, primitive, childish urges, death, revenants, and the ghostly. The familiar contains the unfamiliar and vice versa. The theme of blindness in narratives (Freud 138) or seeing through the other's eyes, like in Hoffman's "Sand-Man," gives the spectre a telepathic quality. Freud lays foundation in this regard: "A person may identify himself with another—unsure of true self" (142). Doublings, doppelgangers are prominent figures in folk tales and fantasy. Repetition compulsion is also key:

> In the unconscious mind we can recognize the dominance of a compulsion to repeat, which proceeds from instinctual impulses ... It is strong enough to override the pleasure principle and lend a demonic character to certain aspects of mental life ... The foregoing discussions have all prepared us for the fact that anything that can remind us of this inner compulsion to repeat is perceived as uncanny. (Freud 145)

Repetition compulsions that we didn't know were repressed are spectral.

The uncanny cradles the inside and outside:

> [A]n uncanny effect often arises when the boundary between fantasy and reality is blurred, when we are faced with the reality of something that we have until now considered imaginary, when a symbol takes on the full function and significance of what it symbolizes, and so forth. (Freud 150–151)

Anachronism is also an important feature: the surmounting of fears and antiquated beliefs reemerge more strongly because they have been so carefully and forcefully buried (Freud 155). The uncanny seems to emanate from inside of us, but this distinction too is blurred. The question Freud ends his essay on is whether the uncanny exists only in art or in real life. Is the uncanny in life different from the uncanny in art? Freud argues that the uncanny must be shared, a common experience, for it to work in art (156). Art can create its own systems of repressions and returns proper to its own specific form and content. Yet, like the uncanny in art and culture, there are common spectres that haunt the multitude. Indeed, art may be an important place to locate the spectres that still have power in modern society at large.

Laura Mulvey links Freud's uncanny with the technological developments of the 19th and early 20th centuries, including photography and film. She does this by showing how the uncanny isn't simply a matter of the old returning to haunt us, but exists within our modern, technologically developed world:

> When he accepts that intellectual uncertainty may be 'a factor' [in the experience of the uncanny], particularly due to its relation to death, Freud quite incidentally suggests a way in which his identification of the uncanny with the 'old' may combine with Jentsch's new mechanical, uncanny. Uncertainty is a bridging concept linking the two. The popular cultures of the uncanny had, for quite some time, created illusions out of

uncertainties particular to the human mind, juxtaposing an uncanny of optical devices and illusions with appearance of ghosts and the spirits of the dead. (*Death* 40)

If Freud's uncanny was a result of the 19th century and a rather masculinist castration anxiety, then how could the 20th century produce spectres? Further, why is there today, in the early 21st century a strong sense of spectrality and the uncanny (Fisher)? What are we even mourning?

Media studies has used the terms of haunting, ghosts, spectres to describe our particular form of communication culture. Debord, Kittler, and Peters have argued that we communicate with ghosts. But this is generally where their analyses of the ghostly dimension stop.[3] What does it mean to communicate with ghosts? How does the definition of the experiential event change within our high-tech society? Derrida takes a position beyond that of media archeology and materialist scholars, like Kittler. Hence *Specters of Marx* offers an important intervention for media studies as it articulates a necessary interdisciplinary relationship between technology and the virtual; Derrida's work on spectrality develops the idea of ghostly media further than in these studies to account for a certain deconstructive spirit of Marxism that includes inheritance, justice, and mourning.

In *Speaking into the Air*, John Durham Peters puts forth an argument about communication as dissemination, the inevitable indeterminacy of all communication. Technological inventions of the 19th century were seen as uncanny and disembodied, and these ideas still carry much weight. Peters constantly reminds us of the inability to control the intention or presence of communication. While Peters takes a macro view of communication from ancient Greece to our attempts to communicate with animals and aliens in contemporary times, Derrida does the same but at a micro level of language and writing, focusing on dissemination within the text itself. Peters claims,

> Humans have long interacted symbiotically with their personal effects, but traces of subjectivity get even more scattered by these new media of dispersion and recording. As Williams James, much in tune with the new audiovisual order, argued, tracts within the material universe can serve as repositories of human personality, whether dead or alive. Media able to capture the flow of time, such as the phonograph and cinema, seemed to vaporize personages into sounds and images. To interact with another person could now mean to read media traces. (142)

Peters agrees with Derrida on the point that communication can never be a meeting of two souls—the risk of indeterminacy is always there (270). We play host to signs—we are not complete, pure beings that can fully and successfully communicate our intentions or desires (257). Peters describes Heidegger's view of communication as a search for authenticity. For Heidegger, we are always thrown into an already meaningful world where the self can be a depository of others, and the goal of philosophy is to rediscover authenticity (16–17). Derrida is content to see communication as a dialogue with ghosts and inauthentic beings. For him, by stressing the failures of communication we arrive at a truer notion of the human subject.

As Harold Innis reminds us in *The Bias of Communication*, every medium has either a prominent space- or time-bias. Time-biased media implies the durability of a specific communicative event, such as gravestones or oral storytelling. Today's ghosts are possibly both time and space binding. They take the form of space-binding media, like photos, films, YouTube, media files shared throughout the globe, but they have the function of binding time or rather jolting us with an out of joint temporality. Spectrality works through space-binding media but has important temporal characteristics. Spectrality is akin to finding a stone from ancient ruins travelling through modern space-binding MP4s. For Peters, video and sound recording technology preserves something of the bodily, sensuous, and temporal dimensions of real life. He adds,

> Media of transmission allow crosscuts through space, but recording media allow jump cuts through time. The sentence of death for sound, image, and experience had been commuted. Speech and action could live beyond their human origins. In short, recording media made the after life of the dead possible in a new way. (144)

In the Victorian mourning era, daguerreotypes captured the spirits of the recently departed (Peters 148). Has anything truly changed since? "Perhaps in a time of video, and tape recording, photo albums and home movies, death seems less final," (148) argues Peters. Appearing in person is no longer a given—we are effectively dispersed like traces on the written page (142).

Derrida's use of psychoanalysis doesn't explore deep-seated trauma or subconscious mechanisms that make meaning hidden, that cause repression, or the return of the repressed, or, even deferral. Derrida draws on psychoanalysis in order to show how these processes are always already at work in the most seemingly conscious and benign forms of communication. Derrida avoids probing deeper into the inner regions of the human psyche. For him, the uncanny, iterability, deferral, etc. are characteristics of all writing systems, including speech: "In fits and starts we have to speak with ghosts, in order to begin to learn to live. The uncanny, interminable rewriting of psychoanalysis: transfer everything that Freud says about the psyche to reading and writing" (Royle 308).

Specters of Marx stretches the psychoanalytic concept of the uncanny to rethink Marx's political philosophy. This time, the uncanny refers to the return of the repressed in all senses of the word—the repression of the past, the lower class, the outcast, etc. What is haunting is the ghost of ideology, and, as Derrida interprets,

Marx proposes that one needs to gain knowledge—to become conscious of one's own ideological construct—in order to accelerate social change. In other words, Marxist revolutionary thinking demands the annihilation of the ideological ghosts in order to achieve true political transformations. Of course, this demand to eradicate the ghosts from the past has ended up with human disasters in all communist worlds.

Fukuyama draws on Marx and Hegel to argue the teleological process of history and the advent of the liberal democracy that coincides with the end of history, an event that has just recently happened, according to him. Fukuyama's contradictory thesis in *The End of History and the Last Man* celebrates the arrival of actual liberal democracy while also downplaying the realities that jeopardize his thesis in favour of the ideal. Derrida argues an unresolvable conflict between idealism and actuality limits the ways the future comes about through inheritance and justice. Derrida emphasizes the ghost at this point because he wants to unravel the binary between actuality and the ideal that has characterized much political philosophy (*Specters* 78–79). The trace will always remain, corrupting any perfect idealism in Hegel for example. And the actual will depend on the non-present remainder, the virtual. The virtual cements this sense of the simultaneous actuality and the ideal, the true and the fictional. The opposition can only be undone by a new experience of the event that Derrida spells out:

> [I]t will not be thought as long as one relies on the simple (ideal, mechanical, or dialectical) opposition of the real presence of the real present or the living present to its ghostly simulacrum, the opposition of the effective or actual (*wirklich*) to the non-effective, inactual, which is also to say, as long as one relies on a general temporality or an historical temporality made up of the successive linking of the presents identical to themselves and contemporary with themselves. (*Specters* 87)

Specters continues developing Derrida's notion of hauntology. In it, Derrida spells out the condition of the postmodernist era: "One does not know: not out of ignorance ... no longer to that which one thinks one knows by the name of knowledge" (*Specters* 5). Hauntology of *Specters* is a continuation of the *Grammatology*. The first time is also the last time. The spectre has a physical/carnal form of the spirit: "As soon as one no longer distinguishes spirit from spectre, the former assumes a body" (Derrida, *Specters* 41). Contra Hegel, ghosts are more than spirit (Peters 116). In Hegel, there is no pure relation to the self. We understand ourselves through others. The Spirit is the harmonious encounter between the self and others:

> [T]he self has no privileged access to itself: it only finds itself post facto or in another self, who has recognized it as a self. Self and other intuit themselves in the same

objective, public stuff—in *Geist*, which consists precisely in this in-betweenness. (Peters 114–115)

Any communication that escapes the community-built, anything that isn't Spirit is potentially ghostly. "[T]here is nothing ghostly about *Geist*," (116) Peters clarifies. *Geist is* our universally agreed upon interpretation of things. Peters continues,

> That works of Spirit speak from the dead and do so invariantly is not a source of horror, as for Socrates, but the basis of cultural continuity. Disembodied intelligence might seem uncannily spectral, but without some kind of intelligence that transcends the body, the dream of communication, after all, would be vain. (117)

The spectre of *Specters* is one that haunts. While it is also a form of Spirit, its power comes from it being excluded. It's Hegel's teleology that gets him into trouble with Derrida and why Fukuyama takes to him so strongly.

Spectrality in *Specters of Marx* is explicitly related to time. Derrida sees three distinct times: temporality, history, and world. The fact that the time is out of joint suggests the world is out of joint, which makes it an ethico-political issue. The disjointness is firstly temporal. Unlike in Marx, Derrida's ghost will always haunt and thus never be cut from actuality. Marx adopted a logocentric view of actuality when he tried to annihilate all ghosts from his political ontology. The spectre will come back or come, for Derrida: "There is nothing contingent about this disjointure, as Hamlet comes to realise—it is as fateful as time, as the ordering of the present" (Buonamano 172). Since Marxism never came, will never come, his ghost will always present itself as a to come, a democracy to come. Haunting is a rich notion, because it ties in with ideas of inheritance and learning how to live.[4] Nick Dyer-Witheford summarizes *Specters*: "Marxism … will manifest a continuing 'spectrality,' an uncanny refusal to stay dead and buried, that is profoundly linked to the increasingly 'spectral,' immaterial, virtual nature of contemporary techno-capitalism" (6). The post-1989 world has witnessed efforts to erase the Marxist past. The mood of erasure ensures that Marxism can start haunting like never before.

What Derrida calls "spectral effects" are different than *Geist* in the traditional sense. Rather than pursuing evidence of the beyond, spectrality explains a specific structure of communication, especially one linked with technology or machine, like photography or television, a communication that is always predetermined to some degree. For him, these effects include, "[T]he new speed of *apparition* (we understand this word in its ghostly sense) of the simulacrum, the synthetic or prosthetic image, and the virtual event, cyberspace and surveillance, the control, appropriations, and speculations that today deploy unheard-of powers" (*Specters* 67). Spectrality takes a step beyond phantomaticity or cinema's illusory qualities to articulate an experience of a certain interpellation, of being regarded by the other and from another time. Without this dimension, spectrality, in fact, doesn't escape the most common sense of the uncanny, nor does it gather the powers of inheritance, mourning, respect, and Law.

Justice isn't contemporaneous. It doesn't hail from the moment. Justice escapes the present. *Re-enter ghost*. Derrida writes evocatively on the nature of speaking to ghosts out of a deep-seated concern for justice:

> One must constantly remember that this absolute evil (which is, is it not, absolute life, fully present life, the one that does not know death and does not want to hear about it) can take place. One must constantly remember that it is even on the basis of the terrible possibility of this impossible that justice is desirable: *through* but also *beyond* right and law. (*Specters* 220)

Specters addresses the neoliberal calls for the death of communism.[5] Derrida states that today we cannot adopt a view of presentism because we are in fact surrounded by ghosts:

> If there is something like spectrality, there are reasons to doubt this reassuring order of presents and, especially, the border between the present, the actual or present reality of the present, and everything that can be opposed to absence, non-presence, non-effectivity, inactuality, virtuality, or even the simulacrum in general, and so forth. There is first of all the doubtful contemporaneity of the present to itself. Before knowing whether one can differentiate between the spectre of the past and the spectre of the future, of the past present and the future present, one must perhaps ask oneself whether the spectrality effect does not consist in undoing this opposition, or even this dialectic, between actual, effective presence and its other. (*Specters* 48)

Spectrality is an outgrowth of deconstruction as the non-present presence confounds philosophy and all rational discourse.

The remainder in Derrida is an unsettling one. Spectres come back from the grave in which they were buried, but reappear without anticipation, as something that has not been totally buried. They reappear as reappearing, as ghosts from the future as well as the past. *Différance* argues language is never stable, guaranteeing some new future meaning and hope. The spectral takes its logic from *différance* in this way: the haunting spectre never joins the present, never makes itself completely available to the moment, defers its meaning until a later date. The difference of the spectre is perhaps due most to its unanticipated, unforeseen nature. To be spectral, the thing must not be anticipated. There is thus something involuntary about it.

The phenomenon of the spectre became much more prominent in Derrida's later writings. As a result of deconstructive thought, the spectre plays an important role in an overall philosophical project that is marked by iterability, indeterminacy, play, and mourning. Spectrality is the act of embracing a non-present remainder to the point where it feels true as it blinds us due to the singularity of the other, the subject. *Marx*, for example.[6] As it concerns the visible, spectrality shows how we can't dominate the visible field. In fact, a part of it controls us, lives in us, rules us, and guides us. Common sense tells us we passively look at images. Derrida disrupts this notion. Spectrality is at once a remainder that is nonetheless present, a type of mourning, a revenant (something that repeats), a gaze, a right of inspection, and a type of (political) inheritance, as defined in the longest study of spectrality that Derrida wrote, *Specters of Marx*.

A trace, such as a photograph or a film, may never take on the nature of inheritance, but there will always be a spectral dimension. This dimension is especially interesting in works of art that foresee their own spectral destiny/capability when they stress certain themes. The works of spectral art are in the wake of a certain post-structuralism, but they are neither wholly postmodern or modern. They are also works of visual mourning. They mourn before the work of mourning truly starts, one might say. Derrida sees the work of mourning in the paintings of Gérard Titus-Carmel. We see it in photographs of the dead and the living-dead. We can also see it throughout Derrida's writing, especially in *The Work of Mourning*. I see it in the films that Derrida made, in Godard's late films, and in the writings on Derrida. The work of mourning is pervasive, but nonetheless highly purposive. The dead are piling up. The work of mourning emerges as an important cultural phenomenon for the late twentieth and early 21st century.

In his critique of spectacle, Guy Debord sees great potential in what he calls styles of negation.[7] *Détournement* rearranges language and signs that are already dominant in society in order to highlight their false logic—something *différance* also seeks to do—and redeploy them for the purposes of revolutionary action. The main strategy of *détournement* is the textual and conscious process of turning common sense into good sense: "The defining characteristic of this use of *détournement* is the necessity for distance to be maintained toward whatever has been turned into an official verity" (Debord 145). The process thaws previously congealed truths, reversing all attempts to persuade via the text, so, the culture of spectacle. In a famous passage, Debord extols the virtues of an unlawful act: plagiarism. He writes, "Ideas improve. The meaning of words has a part in the improvement. Plagiarism is necessary. Progress demands it. Staying close to an author's phrasing, plagiarism exploits his expressions, erases false ideas, replaces them with correct ideas" (145). Debord knows, like Gramsci and Derrida, that to work with pre-established language and genres is the most effective way to put a theory of resistance into *practice*, although these theorists would likely have very different approaches.

In works like *Le gai savoir*, Godard has perhaps come closest to pairing Debordian *détournement* and Derridean *différance*.

Debord claims commodities have a richer life than real people now. Especially today, the spectacular commodity can spread throughout the society in an instant, like a fad (44). In Debord, spectacle is also the extension of money, which Derrida calls a spectral communication. It is also a form of estrangement from the self, since it derives from the world of the commodity. "The spectacle is capital accumulated to the point where it becomes image," (24) Debord writes. He grounds his theory of ideology in material reality (*à la* Althusser). Derrida too is well aware of the spectres of capitalism but sees the communication of spectres as inevitable, whereas many Marxists see it as temporary (Peters 119–127). Marx sees money as an agent corrupting and alienating us from ourselves. It is not surprising that Marx would see this form of representation as inferior to the "real," material thing. But money, a dominant form of "alien" communication, doesn't have an ethical foundation although attempts to give it a retroactive sense of national/economic/teleological value by including portraits of famous people are often made. Spectres circulate on the media of money, but its ubiquity and lack of photorealism deny the full powers of spectrality. We need other cultural forms to explain the kind of spectrality that Derrida is describing.

Spectrality also relates to Horkheimer and Adorno's notion of the dialectic of enlightenment in that the cultural industry within capitalist societies lures people into the content of its artefacts with the promise of reality and harmony, but actually only offers a spectral, addictive relationship with music, film, and television that can never be satiated. Describing the suppression of pleasure that goes along with tantalizing, come-hither imagery, Horkheimer and Adorno famously state, "[The culture industry] reduces love to romance" (111). For the Frankfurt school critics, mass culture, predicated on enlightenment values and technology, enslaved people through a cunning catch-22: "This is the triumph of advertising in the culture industry: the compulsive imitation by consumers of cultural commodities which, at the same time, they recognize as false" (Horkheimer and Adorno 136). The theory of spectrality explains our desire for closeness with the content and subjects of film even as it never delivers on the reality of it. Derrida always maintained the double-sided nature of the spectre, but he wanted to elaborate it and use the concept because of the powerful and relevant way it concerned certain unavoidable imperatives.

In *Right of Inspection*, Derrida argues the rights of inspection are determined by the multiple elements of the photomontage, including genre, sequence, and performance. In this instance, the order creates rules by which one must read a set of images:

> You are free but there are rules, there is a law that assigns the right of inspection [*droit de regard*], you must *observe* these rules that in turn keep you under surveillance. Remain within these limits, this frame, the framework of these frames, the chain of this chain of events. I am serving you notice [*je te mets en demeure*]... (Derrida and Plissart 1)

The right of inspection also concerns Law. *Droit*, in French takes into account this double meaning. It is the authority by which meaning can be derived from the look, gaze, or inspection of the image. While photographs can give us the right of inspection—*here, you may look at me*—this law is also something that can be interiorized but not totally appropriated—*but I may also look at you*. Derrida explains,

> A text of images gives you, as much as it gives its "characters," a right to look, the simple right to look or to appropriate with the gaze, but it denies you that right at the same time: by means of its very apparatus it retains that authority, keeping for itself the right of inspection over whatever discourses you might like to put forth or whatever yarns you might spin about it, and that in fact come to mind before your eyes [*tu vois induire en toi*]. They arise, they grow within you like desire itself, they invade you. (Derrida and Plissart 2)

The law of inspection of the photographic device is coextensive with desire.

Derrida's explanation of the rights of inspection (and indeed spectrality) would seem to draw on the Althusserian notion of interpellation. What came first: the material relations or the representations that mediate those material relations? Althusser defines ideology as "the system of the ideas and representations which dominate the mind of a man or a social group" (149). Althusser sees the base-superstructure theory in Marx as purely metaphorical, and thus he collapses the two. He posits a merely descriptive explanation of capitalist society leaves out the ways in which the state ensures the continuation of the system without the explicit use of violence. Or, to put it another way, a multiplicity of institutions (other than the state) are also interested in the continuation of certain relations of production. None of these institutions are either solely private or public. Bourgeois law attempts to erect this false distinction for the purposes of an absolute authority. Althusser notes, "[T]he Repressive State Apparatus functions 'by violence', whereas the Ideological State Apparatuses *function 'by ideology'*" (138). This is, of course, also Gramsci's insight about the workings of hegemony within civil society. Althusser seeks to explain how the reproduction of the relations of production consistently reoccurs. The Ideological State Apparatuses reveal how this representation happens in a way that is often outside, external to, the moment of labour, where those relations are more concrete and empirical. Althusser locates ideology specifically within the moments of interpellation. He argues, "*[A]ll ideology hails or interpellates concrete individuals as concrete subjects*, by the functioning of the category of the subject" (162).

Spectrality is of visibility, but not quite visible. It is not about what is readily "in sight." The dissymmetry and blindness that are spectral are hinted at in *Specters*, their ideological implications are perhaps best spelled out there, but explored more in-depth in Derrida's films, including *Ghost Dance*, and his project at the Louvre, among other things. The prosthesis of technology elides raw visibility, raw sight, giving us a blind visibility that we incorrectly deem pure, direct, live, or objective. Blindness would indeed give Derrida a new way into deconstruction. Blindness is not a way to deconstruct. It is a precondition that creates the most outstanding examples for showing how the text as a process or the process of writing deconstructs the text itself. Hence Derrida's fascination with blind writers and artists. Our assuredness and reliance on the visible would begin to acknowledge the invisible. In his 1963–1964 *séance* called "Le visible et l'invisible," Derrida stresses we have respect for the invisible only, the law of the phantom; we are before the law only when we are deprived of sight, only when we are *before* the law.

In *Echographies of Television*, a filmed interview Derrida did with Bernard Stiegler, the link between right of inspection and spectre is made even more concretely. He says,

> The specter is not simply this visible invisible that I can see, it is someone who watches or concerns me without any possible reciprocity, and who therefore makes the law when I am blind, blind by situation. The specter enjoys the right of absolute inspection. He is the right of inspection itself. (Derrida and Stiegler 121)

When the spectre has you in its sights, you become blind.[8] It is this aspect of spectrality that will occupy Derrida's thought when he writes *Tourner les mots*. Later, we will see how the blinding effects of spectrality play out in the autobiographical films. Derrida writes,

> The specter is not simply someone we see coming back, it is someone by whom we feel ourselves watched, observed, surveyed, as if by the law: we are 'before the law,' without any possible symmetry, without reciprocity, insofar as the other is watching only us, concerns only us, we who are observing it (in the same way that one observes and respects the law) without even being able to meet its gaze. (Derrida and Stiegler 120)

Writing on the theatre, Derrida repeats, "The visibility of the visible is invisible, the voice isn't visible," words that touch on cinema equally. He adds, "Spectre designates well this indecision between the real and the fictional, which is neither simply an individual or a character or an actor—and it also reminds us of the question of the phantasm in politics" (*Penser* 360).[9] What presents itself as visible, anything in my eyeline, is visible on condition that I/eye don't see its visibility. A trace is visible to me. Its visibility, what it sees, is invisible, thus ensuring it simultaneous secrecy and respect.

Memoirs of the Blind stresses the blindness of the artist, too. When the body moves forward, drawing, making contact with the paper's surface, the movement, production of the trace, inscription isn't seen. Interrupted—ellipsis—this movement (however brief) is total:

> In its originary, pathbreaking [*frayage*] moment, in the *tracing* potency of the *trait*, at the instant when the point at the point of the hand (of the body proper in general) moves forward upon making contact with the surface, the inscription of the inscribable is not seen. Whether it be improvised or not, the invention of the *trait* does not follow, it does not conform to what is presently visible … (Derrida, *Memoirs* 45)

The pencil's blinding effect also points to other premade, technical aspects of artistic creation. Derrida adds, "The heterogeneity between the thing drawn and the drawing *trait* remains abyssal, whether it be between a thing represented and its representation or between the model and the image" (*Memoirs* 45).

In "Trace et archive, image et art," he would later add,

> What fascinates me, is not just the seeing, but the "not seeing." Blindness as a condition of visibility, and of painting and drawing. Sight has always interested me, in philosophy also, not only in the visual arts. But I am not for seeing contra blindness, it is more complicated than that. Blindness is a condition of seeing in a whole tradition that I'm trying to analyze, among other places, in Mémoires d'aveugle. (*Penser* 119)[10]

Derrida asks precisely what happens with the autoportrait or autobiography: the '*punctum caecum*' leads to a blind vision "blinded at this point of 'narcissism,' at the very point where it sees itself looking" (*Memoirs* 53).

The visor effect creates a situation where the gaze of the ghost has the right of inspection over me:

> [T]hrough what Derrida calls the *visor effect* noticeable in the appearance of Old Hamlet's spirit (an effect that is always constitutive as possibility, even if the visor is up), there is a radically asymmetrical distribution of the gaze in the economy of ghostly looking. (Wortham 194)

The spectre comes before us and hence we are responsible for inheriting it. "It de-synchronizes, it recalls us to anachrony," (*Specters* 6) Derrida adds. We are inheritors of the other and we must decide what to do with the ghost's injunction: in the case of *Hamlet* and all spectrality, to correct an injustice. In *Specters of Marx*, this decision will determine our relationship with justice, for the right of inspection that the spectre enjoys can only produce a forceful gaze, but cannot deterministically make us act. This strange economy of invisible visibility is at the root of spectrality. "It is the ghost that regards us, having us in its (invisible) sights," (194) explains Wortham.

The visor effect ensures the impenetrability of the spectre. This means we don't know the content of the spectre, only that we are confronted with it, and therefore by extension with the other. In *Apparitions*, Kas Saghafi writes to this effect:

> It is on the basis of this visor effect that we inherit the law: since we are incapable of looking back at the one who sees us and who makes the law, since the one who issues the injunction cannot be identified, we are delivered over to its voice. Thus the one who says to Hamlet 'I am thy Father's Spirit' can only be taken at his word. This obedience, 'an essentially blind submission to his secret,' is 'a first obedience to the injunction,' the obedience conditioning all others to come. (54)

Photography has the effect of turning the portrayed subject into a spectral other. Saghafi explains, "What Ogier's apparition or the appearance of *Hamlet*'s Ghost would further allow us to say is that the coming of the other is always like the apparition of a ghost" (60). Saghafi is able to say this for many reasons. For him spectrality isn't just about the Marxist inheritance, but more fundamentally the responsibility toward all others (61).

Spectrality is at the nexus point where belief and non-belief overlap. Our society is under the illusion that its knowledge is empirical and scientific. This viewpoint would posit that the light of photochemical process gives us a transparent view of the world, that we can safely account for the history of photography and that the content of the photograph can be connected to facts: dates, people, locations, events, etc. But on the other hand, the photograph also interpellates us in a way that is totally unrelated to the raw facts. Something of the other makes its way into our thoughts and we experience the chill of the revenant. Photography requires us to rely on belief in the origin of the referent.

The use of formulas in Derrida is uncommon, but when they do appear they are pregnant with deconstructive possibilities. When Derrida removes the slash in "Fort/Da" and replaces it with a colon—"Fort:Da"—in *The Post Card*, it is because neither concept in the Freudian context can exist without referring to the other. Fort:Da is understood as a set that cannot be separated. What must return is repetition itself. Likewise, when Derrida offers, "cinema + psychoanalysis = the science of ghosts," the plus marks the supplementarity at root of spectrality. Human consciousness and machinic repetition create together the ghost of spectrality. The risk of this formula is to suggest that everything isn't always already a matter of traces, of cinema. Perhaps for Derrida the "+" isn't simply one of many possible mathematical operators, but the only true operation in a world of supplements. In the end, even when we are in science, we are never being scientific.

Properly speaking, spectrality is a challenge to scientific discourse. Derrida regrets the word "science" in his phrase "Psychoanalysis plus film equals a science of ghosts." He writes,

> [T]here is something which, as soon as one is dealing with ghosts, exceeds, if not scientificity in general, at least what, for a very long time, has modeled scientificity on the real, the objective, which is not or should not be, precisely, phantomatic. It is in the name of the scientificity of science that one conjures ghosts or condemns obscurantism, spiritualism, in short, everything that has to do with haunting and with specters. (Derrida and Stiegler 118)

Death and life blur under its logic, occluding a scientific understanding of it.

Robert Briggs argues that mainstream media determine our perception and experience of events by manipulating space and time:

> Teletechnologies … *make* time. And they *make* space. Or, further: to the extent that teletechnology is not simply a kind of object, a set of particular technologies, but rather that which constitutes and delimits the field of perception and experience, teletechnologies are the very *processes* of making time and making space. (63)

"Teletechnology" creates space and time. It creates space by blurring geographical and political boundaries and identities. Derrida explains,

> [I]f this important frontier is being displaced, it is because the medium in which it is instituted, namely, the medium of the media themselves (news, the press, tele-communications, techno-tele-discursivity, techno-tele-iconicity, that which in general assures and determines the *spacing* of public space, the very possibility of the *res publica* and the phenomenality of the political), this element itself is neither living nor dead, present nor absent: it spectralizes. (*Specters* 63)

It creates time through multiple strategies and techniques that emphasize liveness, presence, and "truth." These strategies may come in the form of live news ticker; voice-over commentary; montage and editing; prepackaged reports; music; cinematic and acting codes, etc.

The purest appeal to presence in visual culture is perhaps live media. Derrida explains "real-time" as a technology that attempts to smooth over the always already divided present. The artifactual consists of a complex mixture of specific institutional, economic, and technological forces working together to deny their own pre-established interventions. Media industries also determine the rhythm of what can be discussed in the public sphere (Derrida and Stiegler 7). Derrida rejects a certain resistance to technology that runs through Romanticism, New Ageism, and Heidegger. He's not just saying media limit and filter what can be said and thought and how thinking is done. "Events (are always already) defined by their essential incompleteness," (62) explains Briggs. The artifactual blurs the ontological line between "reality" and "virtuality." What happens for example to one's experience of the passing of time when filtered through audio-visual recordings and "live" television? Teletechnology, understood as the virtualization of space and time, prohibits us more than ever from opposing presence to its representation, "real time" to "deferred time"… living to the living-dead (Derrida, *Specters* 212). Our experience is transformed profoundly and globally through liveness, which also includes the internet (Derrida and Stiegler 40).

The recording or transmission of live events on television, for example, simply elides the divided present:

> What we call real time is simply an extremely reduced "différance," but there is no purely real time because temporalization itself is structured by a play of retention or of protention and, consequently, of traces: the condition of possibility of the living, absolutely real present is already memory, anticipation, in other words, a play of traces. The real-time effect is itself a particular effect of "différance." This should not lead us to efface or minimize the extraordinary gulf separating what today we call real-time transmission from what had been impossible before. I do not want to try to reduce all of technical modernity to a condition of possibility that it shares with much more ancient times. However, if we are going to understand the originality and the specificity of this technical modernity, we must not forget that there is no such thing as purely real time, that this does not exist in full and pure state. Only on this condition will we understand how technics alone can bring about the real-time "effect." (Derrida and Stiegler 129–130)

Ironically, today we depend on the prosthesis of technology to feel like we are communicating in "real time," that we are witnessing events "live." Cinema, too, can give us this comfortable feeling of transparency that requires us to give up our analytic abilities and self-reflexivity. Quite apart from the writing effects and the 3-second delay in live transmission that actually contradict its ostensible liveness, live TV is more about an ideology of presence and spontaneity than a direct line that taps into world's events. Derrida has written,

> Throughout the new regime of telecommunications, one is no longer where one thought one was. There is sometimes more proximity between a Japanese and a French person than between either of them and his or her neighbour in the same building or village. (Derrida and Roudinesco 97)

The spectral teaches us that one is no longer *when* one thought one was, either.

Notes

1. "Chez Hegel la représentation est le moment toujours central du devenir, le pivot ou le relai essentiel, et précisément dans la structure du déjà pas encore … [E]ntre la religion révélée et la philosophie comme savoir absolu, c'est toujours la représentation qui marque la limite. La représentation est déjà l'étape suivante … Il est arrivé par exemple qu'on traduise phantasia ou

phantasma par représentation, un lexique de Platon le fait par exemple et on le fait couramment pour traduire le corpus stoïcien, mais c'est là supposer anachroniquement que le subjectum et la repraentatio soient possibles et pensables pour des grecs ..."

2. Recently, Pierre Delain has created the online archive Derridex (www.idixa.net) which indexes a significant amount of Derrida's published work. One is able to search Derrida's work by key words, amounting to a kind of "vocabulary of deconstruction."

3. McLuhan saw media as the extensions of *man*, of our senses: TV extends orality, print extends language, and radio extends the ears. Spectrality is the opposite of an extension: it goes inside, plants in us parts of the other, whether as image or sound-trace, from a beyond, from alterity itself. He analysed the relation between media and content, and how content is shaped by the form. Without teletechnology there wouldn't be a proliferation of spectral sights and sounds today. He insisted that media was the message and put all emphasis on the media, instead of the meaning found in the content-form nexus. If spectrality is the suspense between now and then, presence and absence, then isn't it also the tension between content and its container? As a challenge to media transparency, deconstruction stresses the importance of examining both.

4. The democracy to come relates to messianism and some challenging questions follow. Messianism is a promise. What is a promise without any metaphysical attributes? The meaning of the sign is perhaps one that gains something messianic only in the future. Does messianism try to prevent the play of *différance*? Or is it a *différance* that only becomes meaningful because of the way it always means more in times to come?

5. *Specters of Marx* sets the stage for the return of the Marxist subject who was traditionally under-developed in Marx proper (Read). Ironically though the subject returns as spectre. By emphasizing spectrality Derrida once again makes the question of the subject in Marx partly obscured.

6. For more on the singularity of the other in photography, see Saghafi, 87.

7. Debord argues for the greater revolutionary potential of *détournement*: "The revolution organization must necessarily constitute an integral critique of society—a critique, that is to say, which refuses to compromise with any form of separated power and which is globally against every aspect of alienated social life" (88). There is also a parallel here with Benjamin's "The Author as Producer," where the point is to allow each citizen to "inscribe their thought upon practice" (89) and show that their consciousness comes from themselves and not some higher entity, author or intellectual leader.

8. In logocentric thought, blindness occurs whenever we reach for the supplement instead of the "real thing." Agriculture is privileged over mining in Rousseau. "Mine-blindness" results from turning away from natural, living plants. Derrida reminds us in *Of Grammatology* of the irony of the supplement: "Blindness thus produces that which is born at the same time as society: the languages, the regulated substitution of signs for things, the order of the supplement. One goes *from blindness to the supplement*. But the blind person cannot see, in its origin, the very thing he produces to supplement his sight. *Blindness to the supplement* is the law. And especially blindness to its concept. Moreover, it does not suffice to locate its functioning in order to *see* its meaning. The supplement has no sense and is given to no intuition. We do not therefore make it emerge out of its strange penumbra. We speak its reserve" (149).

9. "[L]a visibilité du visible est invisible, la voix n'est pas visible non plus ...[Spectre] désigne bien cette indécision entre le réel et le fictionnel, ce qui n'est ni simplement individu ou personage ou acteur—et cela rappelle aussi à la question du phantasme en politique."

10. "Ce qui me fascine, ce n'est pas seulement le voir, c'est le 'ne pas voir.' La cécité comme condition de la visibilité, et de la peinture et du dessin. La question de la vue m'a intéressé depuis toujours, dans la philosophie aussi, non seulement dans les arts visuels. Mais je ne suis pas pour le voir contre l'aveuglement, c'est plus compliqué. L'aveuglement est la condition du voir dans toute une tradition que j'essaie d'analyser, entre autres lieux, dans Mémoires d'aveugle."

Bibliography

Althusser, Louis. "Ideology and Ideological State Apparatuses." *Lenin and Philosophy, and Other Essays*. Trans. Ben Brewster. New York: Monthly Review Press, 1971. 127–186.

Benjamin, Walter. *The Work of Art in the Age of Its Technological Reproducibility and Other Writings on Media*. Ed. Michael W. Jennings, Brigid Doherty, Thomas Y. Levin. Cambridge, MA: Belknap Press of Harvard University Press, 2008.

Bennington, Geoffrey, and Jacques Derrida. *Jacques Derrida*. Trans. Geoffrey Bennington. Chicago, IL: University of Chicago Press, 1993.

Briggs, Robert. "Teletechnology." *Jacques Derrida: Key Concepts*. Ed. Claire Colebrook. Abingdon, Oxon: Routledge, 2015.

Buonamano, Roberto. "The Economy of Violence: Derrida on Law and Justice." *Ratio Juris* 11.2 (June 1998): 168–179.

Debord, Guy. *The Society of the Spectacle*. New York: Zone Books, 1994.

Derrida, Jacques. "Le visible et l'invisible" *Séances* notes. 1963–1964. Jacques Derrida Archives 1949–2004. L'Institut Mémoires de l'édition contemporaine, Basse-Normandie, France.

———. "La Représentation" *Séances* notes. 1980–1981. Jacques Derrida Archives 1949–2004. L'Institut Mémoires de l'édition contemporaine, Basse-Normandie, France.

———. *Margins of Philosophy*. Trans. Alan Bass. Chicago, IL: University of Chicago Press, 1982.

———. *Memoirs of the Blind: The Self-Portrait and Other Ruins*. Trans. Pascale-Anne Brault and Michael Naas. Chicago, IL: University of Chicago Press, 1993.

———. *Of Grammatology*. Trans. Gayatri Chakravorty Spivak. Baltimore and London: The Johns Hopkins University Press, 1997.

———. *Specters of Marx: The State of the Debt, the Work of Mourning, and the New International*. Trans. Peggy Kamuf. New York and London: Routledge, 2006.

———. *Penser à ne pas voir: Écrits sur les arts du visible 1979–2004*. Paris: Éditions de la différence, 2013.

Derrida, Jacques, and Bernard Stiegler. *Echographies of Television*. Trans. Jennifer Bajorek. Cambridge: Polity Press, 2002.

Derrida, Jacques, and Elisabeth Roudinesco. *For What Tomorrow …* Trans. Jeff Fort. Stanford, CA: Stanford University Press, 2004.

Derrida, Jacques, and Marie-François Plissart. *Right of Inspection*. Trans. David Wills. New York: Monacelli Press, 1998.

Dyer-Witheford, Nick. *Cyber-Marx: Cycles and Circuits of Struggle in High-Technology Capitalism.* Urbana: University of Illinois Press, 1999.

Fisher, Mark. *Ghosts of My Life: Writings on Depression, Hauntology and Lost Futures.* Alresford, Hants: Zero Books, 2014.

Freud, Sigmund. *The Uncanny.* Trans. David McLintock. London: Penguin, 2003.

Fukuyama, Francis. *The End of History and the Last Man.* New York: The Free Press, 1992.

Horkheimer, Max, and Theodor W. Adorno. *Dialectic of Enlightenment: Philosophical Fragments.* Trans. Edmund Jephcott. Stanford, CA: Stanford University Press, 2002.

Innis, Harold. *The Bias of Communication.* Toronto: University of Toronto Press, 1964.

McLuhan, Marshall. *Understanding Media: The Extensions of Man.* Cambridge: MIT Press, 1994.

Mulvey, Laura. *Death 24x a Second: Stillness and the Moving Image.* London: Reaktion Books, 2006.

Naas, Michael. *Miracle and Machine: Jacques Derrida and the Two Sources of Religion, Science, and the Media.* New York: Fordham University Press, 2012.

Peters, John Durham. *Speaking into the Air: A History of the Idea of Communication.* Chicago and London: University of Chicago Press, 1999.

Read, Jason. *The Micro-Politics of Capital: Marx and the Prehistory of the Present.* Albany: State University of New York Press, 2003.

Royle, Nicholas. *The Uncanny.* New York: Routledge, 2003.

Saghafi, Kas. *Apparitions—Of Derrida's Other.* New York: Fordham University Press, 2010.

Wortham, Simon Morgan. *The Derrida Dictionary.* London and New York: Continuum, 2010.

CHAPTER TWO

1ˢᵗ *Séance*: Photography's Suspense Effect

Photography is recognized in Naas, Saghafi, and Derrida as a form of spectrality and *différance* in its structure, delay playing a major role. Cinema itself is haunted by stillness, and hence contains the same attributes these theorists observe in photography. What makes film spectral is the photography that is its basis. The technical apparatus shows itself when film slows down or repeats itself. Delay casts light on the tracing machine at work. Delay causes suspense between the now of the viewing and the time of the recording. It is this elementary suspense that creates a tension prompting us to return to an origin that oscillates between presence and absence, which is the basis of spectrality and also "archive fever." In this chapter, I explore deconstructive approaches to film in terms of the employment of photography's characteristic delay effects that postpone meaning. As Laura Mulvey persuasively shows we can actively stop cinema and allow its dead, uncanny images to shape and haunt us.

For photography and film scholars, like Barthes, Eduardo Cadava, André Bazin, Gilberto Perez, and Garrett Stewart, photography is imbricated with the powerful activities of mourning. Derrida's philosophical commitment to photography, the very basis of cinema according to André Bazin, must be acknowledged. In several works, such as "The Death of Roland Barthes," *Athens, Still Remains*, and *Copy, Archive, Signature*, Derrida offers important insights into photography and the photographic arts in general. In *Camera Lucida*, Barthes defines the *studium* as the intended, culturally produced (or coded) dimension of photography. The *punctum*, on the other hand, is never coded. The *punctum* speaks to me, concerns me, and therefore contains the power of the spectre. In "The Deaths of Roland Barthes," Derrida deconstructs the opposition between the *studium* and *punctum* as developed by Barthes: "[The *punctum*] belongs to [the photograph] without belonging to it and is unlocatable within it; it is never inscribed in the homogeneous objectivity of the framed space but instead inhabits or, rather, haunts it" (*Work* 41). As a supplement, the *punctum* is haunted by the possibility of repetition, *studium*, and both categories are affected by photography's death effect, making the *punctum* very much a product of culture along with the *studium*. As a powerful writing performance, photography produces traces of things or places that have the potential to return to us like ghosts. Derrida continues, "We are prey to the ghostly power of the supplement; it is this unlocatable site that gives rise to the *specter*" (*Work* 41).[1]

What spurred Barthes on in writing *Camera Lucida* was a desire to recapture some of the closeness he felt for his recently departed mother. It is the medium's preservative dimension that attracted him so much. This is also what attracted Derrida to photography to some extent: "[Photography] implies the 'return of the dead' in the very structure of both its image and the phenomenon of its image. This does not happen in other types of images or discourses" (*Work* 53). Focusing on the transparency of the medium, Barthes is able to shed some of the cynicism of the semiologist and enter into a more direct relation with the real world. For Barthes photography gives us that *option*. Visibility of others (and ourselves) is actually the unspoken thesis of the book. Why else is the inclusion of photographs of various people (and especially their faces) so essential to Barthes' *method*?[2] Barthes trusts the photograph and gives up a degree of scepticism: certain historical truths become clearer through this "new, somehow experiential order of proof" (*Camera* 79). The camera picks up characteristics that the novel cannot. The camera mechanically captures these details and thus enlarges our understanding of the diversity there is to be found in the world. There is no denying the multiplicity of people and histories. The contingency of the photographic image somehow awaits their inclusion. The only thing in the way is censorship of all kinds. Derrida would say we only ever internalize the other's gaze, but never the other's true self.

Philippe Ariès describes two distinct attitudes toward death that mark the shift from the middle ages to the present:

> The first, the oldest, the longest held, and the most common one, is the familiar resignation to the collective destiny of the species and can be summarized by the phrase, *Et moriemur*, and we shall all die. The second, which appeared in the twelfth century, reveals the importance given throughout the entire modern period to the self, to

one's own existence, and can be expressed by another phrase, *la mort de soi*, one's own death. (55)

Death has appeared in traditional and ritualistic art throughout history, but as burial rites and other traditions change and new art forms take hold, death and dying and their representations must be reinterpreted. Contemporary artists and scholars have commonly chosen photography as the medium that is intricately connected to death. "Death is the *eidos* of [the] Photograph," (*Camera* 15) wrote Barthes who theorized most notably on the relationship between death and photography. Barthes sees the photograph's stillness as the death of a moment and a powerful prophet of the inevitable deaths awaiting us all:

> In the Photograph, Time's immobilization assumes only an excessive, monstrous mode: Time is engorged ... That the Photograph is 'modern', mingled with our noisiest everyday life, does not keep it from having an enigmatic point of actuality, a strange stasis, the stasis of an *arrest*. (*Camera* 91)

If photography is death, then death itself must share an important and unique relationship with the photograph. Describing a photograph of a convicted man, Barthes defines death as the logic of the photograph:

> [T]he *punctum* is: *he is going to die*. I read at the same time: *This will be* and *this has been*; I observe with horror an anterior future of which death is the stake ... Whether or not the subject is already dead, every photograph is this catastrophe. (*Camera* 96)

Mulvey sees the photograph as the basis of cinema, thus bringing in all the characteristics of arrest, death. Mulvey shows how death is intertwined with cinema at many levels (narratological and technological), as her study emphasizes the power of delay in cinema.

In *Athens, Still Remains*, Derrida considers a series of photographs of Athens by Jean-François Bonhomme, many of them depicting the city's ruins and commercial spaces. The word *demeure*, as well as signifying "staying" and "home," means a special kind of stasis that is specific to photography. Instead of relating the theme of stasis or death to a Bazinian mummification, as would traditionally be done in studies of death and photography, Derrida draws from a saying or thought that came to him one day in Athens: We owe ourselves to death or *Nous nous devons à la mort*. The activities of mourning are paramount to Derrida's conception of the photographs. Athens is a city that dies a little more each day, a city whose ruins are aplenty and that seems to invite the work of the photographer-as-archivist. Delay is an inbuilt feature of photography, as Derrida conceives it. The delay that characterizes the activities of the photographer, such as the delay of setting up the shot before the click of the camera and the waiting that occurred after the picture was taken, waiting for the photo to be developed, and the delay of the photograph itself, the way it holds our attention, seems to colour the entire photographic enterprise with the logic of mourning. Derrida's interdisciplinary approach in this short book finds the philosopher incorporating autobiographical details and the technology of photography into his philosophical argument. He regrets that he came to Athens late in life: "But a delay, these days, is something I always love as what gives me the most to think, more than the present moment, more than the future and more than eternity, a delay before time itself" (*Athens* 17).

In *Copy, Archive, Signature*, Derrida confronts the latest frontiers of photography, including digital cameras and live TV, and pays greater attention to technology as a determining force of the context of photography. Although the book reproduces a very short interview, it is full of fascinating insights on photography, and it demonstrates how deconstructive readings of new visual media can continue to be forged. The interview starts with a description of what makes digital photography different from film-based photography. It is argued that the recording and producing moments of photography are now combined under a single performative act, turning photography into an endeavour akin to Photoshop, one that instantly archives itself and makes the technological act just as important as the artistic one.

Derrida's interest in the technological component of delay harkens back to his explanations of supplement and the apparatus of writing, although the technological dimension actually becomes more accentuated in later years. Naas also suggests he becomes most interested in it on the occasion of these shorter pieces on photography ("When it All Suddenly Clicked"). The photographic project is already marked by indeterminacy, and lack of aura, as Derrida will go on to show. He reminds us that even before photography, perception is a kind of photographic operation:

> We can no longer oppose perception and technics; there is no perception before the possibility of prosthetic iterability; and this mere possibility marks, in advance, both perception and the phenomenology of perception. In perception there are already operations of selection, of exposure time, of filtering, of development; the psychic apparatus functions also *like*, or *as*, an apparatus of inscription and of the photographic archive. (*Copy* 14–15)

Throughout the book, Derrida will make many similar insights. "As in 'Freud and the Scene of Writing,' it is the technical apparatus that reveals to us that there is already technicity in the form of selection in the putatively pre-technical realm of perception," ("When it All Suddenly Clicked" 95) Naas stresses. Photography scholars cannot read this book without experiencing the regret that the founder of deconstruction didn't write more on the visual arts and media. We are left with a few short works by a thinker who wanted to theorize media in a philosophically rigorous way.

Derrida wrote multiple pieces on photography from the mid-1980s onward. Photography becomes a key topic in late Derrida, as demonstrated by Naas, who argues,

> [T]he fundamental notions of deconstruction itself could come to light only in a time that was not contemporaneous with itself by means of the supplement of psychoanalysis or the technical inventions of photography, as if the archives of deconstruction had to be open not just in fact but in principle to an invention that would make us rethink the very nature of deconstruction "itself." ("When it All Suddenly Clicked" 83)

Delay is an important part of both deconstruction and increasingly in film theory. Naas argues photography powerfully exemplifies the deferrals of *différance*. Photography seems to privilege the deferrals so important to *différance*'s movement of signs and meaning:

> I would like to argue photography and psychoanalysis concur, that is, come together, emerge or develop together, around a notion of time as deferral, non-concurrence, or non-simultaneity—all ways of describing what Derrida will have called from the very beginning différance or supplementarity. Photography and psychoanalysis would thus concur in time over a certain non-concurrence in space and time, a non-concurrence that, I would like to suggest in conclusion, is also the very temporality of deconstruction and the archive. ("When it All Suddenly Clicked" 82)

The metaphor of the mystic writing pad isn't just a metaphor in Freud, according to Derrida. Freud can't develop an argument of psychic apparatus without it. Naas shows how metaphoricity, technology, supplement, representation, death, photography, and camera are grouped together in Derrida's thought. Indeed these concepts have been reinforcing each other in Derrida since *Of Grammatology*. Naas continues,

> It is on the basis of this rethinking of metaphor and technology, on the basis of what might be called the irreducible metaphoricity of discourse, that we might want to bring to read Derrida's works of the 1980s and 1990s on photography. ("When it All Suddenly Clicked" 91)

In short, photography allows Naas to re-read delay—the belated "now" of deconstruction—from the very beginning of Derrida's works. He sums it up, "[M]etaphor, now, as a machine" ("When it All Suddenly Clicked" 90).

Naas argues deconstruction can be understood better through consideration of photographic technologies. Cinema and photography allow the detail to be magnified. This is also a goal of psychoanalysis. In "When it All Suddenly

Clicked," Naas observes, "Derrida asks whether the supposed life and spontaneity of memory does not depend upon repetition, material supplement of the machine ... that is ... death" (90). Naas' argument is that deconstruction will only come into light once it has taken photography seriously. "We should not assume we know what photography is," (92) he claims. Naas' intervention is important because it doesn't represent another attempt to apply deconstruction onto an art or technology without being sure what deconstruction or philosophy gets in return. He describes a cyclical relationship wherein deconstruction becomes more tenable as a result of photographic technology: "[I]t is the very notion of deferral ... that makes it impossible to say that temporality simply comes before the metaphor of photography ..." (93). Photography as a metaphor for deconstruction was always there. This is why Naas argues, "In time there is already photography" (94). Naas maintains Derrida arrived at this conclusion early in his writings. A new invention reveals to us what already was there, a technicity or structure, like Freud's mystic writing pad or writing in "Plato's Pharmacy." Naas' contribution allows us to talk of the image as *différance*. Images can be a matter of *différance*. For the first delay, before the camera's click, already contains an image. The image is already an image before it's an image. There are spectres, foreknowing before the image is taken. This understanding of time is true to deconstruction, but most film theory doesn't even begin to grapple with the consequences of *différance* even though cinema and deconstruction now share important common realities.

To summarize a large amount of recent post-structuralist theorization on the topic, every photograph is in a sense haunted by the absence of its referent. When the camera clicks and the photograph is taken, the death of the moment is inscribed within it. Photography creates temporally out of joint spectres, ghostly others, like Hamlet's father's ghost, that are no longer connected to their origins, but exist as images, apparitions. Death is never a settled matter in Derrida. Why are some images more haunting than others? In war photography, for example, we internalize the ghost of a dying man who will keep on living both outside and inside of us. When the referent gets further and further away from the image, the greater the haunting. Saghafi notes,

> In photography the referent is not renounced but is *held* in abeyance. Even though this suspension entails putting off, deferring, and delaying the encounter with the absolute referent, the wholly other, a suspended relation is still maintained with the referent in this process of placing it in quotation marks. This suspended relation denotes *suspense* (the state of being suspended, of awaiting determination or a decision that is *pending*) but also *dependence* on the referent (a hanging onto, a reliance on it). While there is no direct access to it, the referent is still desired and reference is maintained. (89)

When Derrida describes the uncanny experience of encountering Pascale Ogier's ghost in *Echographies of Television*, it is vital that he stress how far apart her image and her actual self were: he saw *Ghost Dance*, the film in which he stars along with Ogier, at the behest of his students, years later, in Texas, and, finally, after her death. In terms of joining up with the referent, the image will always be in a state of delay. The ability of the photographic arts to bring about the return of the other's gaze that we then internalize is quite striking and one of the ways visual culture allows and prompts us to mourn.[3]

Naas argues that photography privileges the movement of *différance* (the deferring and differing of meaning in deconstruction) because of the way photography's delay effects create potential endless interpretations of the present moment or the detail. Indeed, the delay before the picture is taken potentially creates a spectre that was never not part of the image. A paradox exists at the heart of Derrida's concept of the spectre: mainly that spectrality points to *différance* and yet it haunts through its non-present remainder. Meaning is differed but that only makes the sign stronger. This is the paradoxical, unsteady foundation on which deconstruction rests:

> Death is the movement of differance to the extent that that movement is necessarily finite. This means that differance makes the opposition of presence and absence possible. Without the possibility of differance, the desire of presence as such would not find its breathing-space. That means by the same token that this desire carries in itself the destiny of its non-satisfaction. Differance produces what it forbids, makes possible the very thing that it makes impossible. (*Of Grammatology* 143)

While the meaning of the detail in photography is deferred, spectrality makes the past reappear only to die again (Saghafi 77). The spectre and *différance* are both produced out of the same deconstructive logic. The sign of *différance*, haunted by its own chains of supplements, forever delays finality, and spectrality's oscillation between presence and absence always delays access to its origin. *Différance*, however, would seem to better fit the workings of the written text or phonetic language much more than spectrality, which appears designed for the image and sound, perhaps due to their bodily dimensions. *Différance* and spectrality mock our search for transcendence or source. Spectrality haunts because it is other (another time, another subjectivity, etc.), *because we are in the process of archiving it*, because it must first appear as other, sometimes even monstrous. Derrida argues,

> [In montage, the] chimera becomes a possibility. If there is an art of photography (beyond that of determined genres, and thus in an almost transcendental space), it is found here. Not that it suspends reference, but that it indefinitely defers a certain type of reality, that of the perceptible referent. (Derrida and Plissart 35)

If there is such a thing as Derridean film theory, it must emphasize the technical nature of the medium while developing subject positioning and ideology critique approaches. Brunette and Wills, utilizing Derrida's use of the word "hymen" from "The Double Session," argue realism and mimesis are privileged in the cinema. They write, "[S]imply by doubling its referent, like a mirror, it exposes both its pure supplementarity and its profound difference, its potential deformation of that referent" (*Screen/Play* 84). And further:

> [W]e shall not hesitate to call cinema the deconstruction of the mimetic operation rather than the confirmation of it, and it is in this sense that the screen can be called a hymen. In the space of the hymen/screen/mirror, a site that marks the inside of the apparatus from its outside, one encounters the limit to which realist representation can extend itself and the frail support for an operation that traverses it without rending it. (*Screen/Play* 85)

A membrane displaying traces of light,

> the screen becomes not the site of the consecration of that former metaphysically oriented or motivated operation but rather its marginal or liminal support. Its supposed diaphanous quality then results not so much from its being an imperfect window upon the world but from its functioning as membrane, locus of relay and articulation, as well as system of protection involving its own abolition. In other words, the screen must both be present and obscured, or absent, for its effect to be realized. (*Screen/Play* 79)

In "Cinema-Graphia: Eisenstein, Derrida, and the Sign of Cinema," Laura R. Oswald develops the notion of cinema-graphia to account for the similarities between writing and cinema. This notion emphasizes the self-reflexively graphic nature of the medium. She writes,

> [C]inema-graphia designates a theory and a practice of cinema focused on relations between elements of the enunciation, *across* the frame. The logocentric space of the photographic image is thus superseded by the precarious movement of meaning and being in the space-time of cinema-graphia. (Brunette and Wills, *Deconstruction* 250)

In other words, Oswald pays greater attention to the image's relation to other images, to montage, and to the image or shot's relation to the other movement and writing effects of the film. Her main example of cinema-graphia is from Eisenstein (Brunette and Wills, *Deconstruction* 255–259). While the Soviet filmmaker's approach to montage stresses the importance of synthesis of two ideas or shots, his filmmaking gestures toward deconstructive logic. Often in Eisenstein, a shot is supposed to carry one meaning. The combination of two shots (1 + 1 = 3) produces the intended third meaning. However, this type of montage compels us to understand the shot as a matter of deferred meaning. The meaning of the shot comes later, after it is presented: only once the image of a cow being slaughtered is added next to the image of workers being trampled upon do we get a fuller picture of the capitalist's subjugation of the working class.

Juxtaposition is key to Oswald's reading and importation of Derrida into the study and practise of film. As she sees it, there is deconstructive potential in montage:

> If we were to locate a 'Derridian' gesture within Eisenstein's poetics, we would have to focus on the extent to which Eisenstein seeks to suspend closure between cinematic figuration and its meaning in order to delay indefinitely the full presence of a signified to consciousness. (Brunette and Wills, *Deconstruction* 257)

Oswald finds such uses of montages in Tarkovsky and Resnais, which she only briefly mentions. She describes a scene in *The Mirror* (Soviet Union, 1975) where a lingering shot of the mother cuts to Aloysha who appears to be in another space/time, but this discovery is only gradual and is marked by a shift from colour photography to monochrome. Writing on the scene, she claims,

> The movement of the narrative point of view dislocates the position of spectating I/eye in turn. The spectator no sooner finds a footing in the events of the fiction than the editing breaks the terms of scopic identification and opens up yet another space-time and yet another locus in which the spectator must insert himself or herself. The intrication of narrating and spectating subjectivities never quite achieves a coherent unity in the present and presence of the film image, but follows a movement without origin, present, or presence, a movement that perpetually postpones the closure of I and eye to an unlocatable future-past. The endless movement between desire and fulfillment, between anticipation and remembrance in *The Mirror* is dictated by the film frame marking junctures between vision and blindness, between reality seen and imaginary scene in film discourse. (Brunette and Wills, *Deconstruction* 262–263)

This sense of unsure footing ensures that the viewer interacts with the image, that is, apparatus.

Apparatus theories conceive of cinema as a host of technical practises, from the production to the reception, that affect viewer psychology. Apparatus theories were de rigueur in the 1970s when film theory was infused with Marxist and Lacanian political and cultural worldviews (see Rosen). The technical aspect of the medium and how a subject gets positioned were always emphasized. Apparatus theory deals with the mechanics of the cinematic experience. In "Ideological Effects of the Cinematographic Apparatus," Jean-Louis Baudry looks for a way to explain the ideological effects of the apparatus by expanding upon Freud's mystic writing pad. Baudry stresses the minimal ideological effects of recording raw reality. Cinema is a mode of representation that he calls "*perspectiva artificalis*":

> [D]o the instruments (the technical base) produce specific ideological effects, and are these effects themselves determined by the dominant ideology? In which case, concealment of the technical base will also bring about an inevitable ideological effect. Its inscription, its manifestation as such, on the other hand, would produce a knowledge effect, as actualization of the work process, as denunciation of ideology, and as critique of idealism. (Baudry 288)

Baudry suggests filmic inscriptions (framing, editing, depth of field) offer clues to the kind of ideological effects that are produced by the cinema.

The way the camera frames the image according to Western aesthetics and the way it simulates motion are suspect to Baudry:

> Monocular vision, which as Pleynet points out is what the camera has, calls forth a sort of play of 'reflection.' Based on the principle of a fixed point by reference to which the visualized objects are organized, it specifies in return the position of the 'subject,' the very spot it must necessarily occupy. (289)

The subject is being formed here through the technological apparatus. This has implications on what we call evidence, because according to apparatus theory everything that is filmed is destined to be "read" intelligibly by a subject, and not simply taken for granted. To many viewers today, the video of the Rodney King beating, probably shows an African American man being excessively beaten by the police. Memorably, the trial resulted in the police officers being acquitted of the charges against them. Why? As Judith Butler shows, even unedited documentary video is interpreted ("Endangered/Endangering"). The implication is that King's attorney had relied too much on a common belief that documentary film equalled reality—representation is mistaken as reality. Indeed, had his lawyers shaped the jury's interpretation of the video, there might have been a different outcome.[4]

Cinema is very much like a system of writing in that it inscribes difference (different shot units) similarly to writing, but in film the differentiated moment is covered over by movement:

> On the one hand, the optical apparatus and the film permit the marking of difference (but the marking is already negated, we have seen, in the constitution of the perspective image with its mirror effect). On the other hand, the mechanical apparatus both selects the minimal difference and represses it in projection, so that meaning can be constituted; it is at once direction, continuity, movement. The projection mechanism allows the different elements (the discontinuity inscribed by the camera) to be suppressed, bringing only the relation into play. (Baudry 291)

If continuity and movement hold sway over film's access to truth and reality, then deconstruction would seek to stop the film dead in its tracks. Louise Burchill uses Baudry as a stand-in for Derrida in her essay "Derrida and the (Spectral) Scene of Cinema." Particularly relevant in Burchill is her description of Derrida's deconstruction of Husserl's phenomenology as a series of now's. Derrida maintains the present is divisible, as opposed to Husserl (Burchill 167). The implication of this for film is that difference underlies the medium.

The object and subject come together within Baudry's theory, making objectivity the result of subjective forces:

> There is a phantasmatization of objective reality (images, sounds, colors)—but of an objective reality which, limiting its powers of constraint, seems equally to augment the possibilities or the power of the subject. As it is said of consciousness—and in point of fact we are concerned with nothing less—the image *of* something; it must result from a deliberate act of consciousness [*visée intentionelle*]. (Baudry 292)

The phantasmatization of reality must therefore mean a kind of conjuring, a faux subject. Film feigns transcendence, in other words. The apparatus, not just the content, facilitates film's meaning. He writes,

> Ultimately, the forms of narrative adopted, the 'contents' of the image, are of little importance so long as an identification remains possible … It is an apparatus destined to obtain a precise ideological effect, necessary to the dominant ideology: creating a phantasmatization of the subject, it collaborates with a marked efficacy in the maintenance of idealism. (Baudry 295)

The viewer is interpolated as the transcendental subject. The cinema, for Baudry, is a support of ideology in the final analysis.

Derrida argues that the ostensible realism of the photographic referent has undergone a seismic shift with the advent of the digital, but emphasizes that the relation between the referent and the image has always been complicated:

> Reference is complex; it is no longer simple, and in that time subevents can occur, differentiations, micrological modifications giving rise to possible compositions, dissociations, and recompositions, to "effects," if you like, to artifices that definitively break with the presumed phenomenological naturalism that would see in photographic technology the miracle of a technology that effaces itself in order to give us a natural purity, time itself, the unalterable and un-iterable experience of a pretechnical perception (as if there were any such thing). (*Copy* 8–9)

Photography makes the moment die and live simultaneously:

> [H]owever artful the photographer may be, whatever his or her intervention or style, there is a point where the photographic act is not an artistic act, a point where it passively records, and this poignant passivity would be the chance of this relation with death; it captures a reality that is there, that will have been there, in an undecomposable now. (*Copy* 9)

The irrefutable existence of the referent—which is possibly at its fullest expression in cinema, in the flow of life—always rubs up against the death that technics provides. However untouched or devoid of "effects" the photographic image may be, the death effect will always bring technics to mind. Spectrality comes on the scene precisely to offer the hope necessary to put life back into stillness and delay.

Derrida is perhaps more aware of the mechanics of the apparatus than Baudry. Cinema viewers face the prospect of internalization more than pure identification, that is to say, assimilation of every cinematic element (actor, light, sound, etc.). Film doesn't succeed in erecting the pure form of identification spelled out by Baudry, and one might say disembodiment is the greatest source of phantasmic haunting. Derrida stresses the role of invention in the photographic scene: "[T]here is a concept of photography as the simple recording of the other as he was, as he appeared there, but it is immediately contaminated by invention in the sense of production, creation, productive imagination" (*Copy* 43). The apparatus doesn't simply guide our perception of the other, but, according to Derrida, helps create it: "One produces the other there where he is not; therefore I can manipulate a photograph, intervene, transform the referent: I invent him, then, in the sense in which one invents what is not there" (*Copy* 43). There is no strict division between photography as a technological act and its experience (*Copy* 44). Derrida's apparatus theory stresses the invention of the other by means of technics.

Mulvey's *Death 24x a Second* takes Derrida a step further in that she actually seeks out moments of delay in film history and uses new digital technology to stop film in order to analyze it. *Death 24x a Second* provides a fresh, theoretically-grounded methodology that allows artists and spectators to use digital technologies to study film differently: "Digital technology enables a spectator to still a film in a way that evokes the ghostly presence of the individual celluloid frame," (26) she explains.[5] Mulvey credits the avant-garde for revealing the stillness of cinema:

> The illusion of movement is necessarily extended within time, in duration. A still frame when repeated creates an illusion of stillness, a freeze frame, a halt in time. Stillness may evoke a 'before' for the moving image as filmstrip, as a reference back to photography or to its own original moment of registration. Although the projector reconciles the opposition and the still frames come to life, this underlying stillness provides cinema with a secret, with a hidden past that might or might not find its way to the surface. (*Death* 67)

Like Derrida, Mulvey argues stillness is related to death, while movement is related to story and life. Even an image that is repeated ceaselessly, like the one in *The Limey* of Wilson (Terence Stamp) sitting in the airplane, potentially carries with it the characteristic of death and delay that are essential to Mulvey's analysis of film. Stillness can create this sense of delay and the uncanny. Mulvey doesn't seem bound by disciplinary obligations either. In her study, she draws on history, Freud, theories of technology, and her own experiences as a film viewer to describe cinema's underlying reliance on delay and death.

Commenting on the scene in *Psycho* (dir. Hitchcock, US, 1960) following Marion's (Janet Leigh) death, she writes,

> The stillness of the 'corpse' is a reminder that the cinema's living and moving bodies are simply animated stills and the homology between stillness and death returns to haunt the moving image ... Looking closely at the film, her stillness is so deathly that it almost seems as though Hitchcock had substituted a still photograph for the living actress. (*Death* 88)

And modern ways of viewing (moving) images have only amplified this tendency. The single still shot of Marion marks the end of a fairy-tale narrative and the beginning of a detective story, occupying both genres at once. While Mulvey could have developed this idea of delay even further—she could have compared moments of stillness and movement featuring Marion to see how the theme of death played out therein—her study makes a key insight that brings together deconstruction and film theory through the notion of delay. Like the film scholar, video artists have also harnessed these technologies in order to deconstruct the opposition between stillness and movement. Douglas Gordon's *24-Hour Psycho* (UK, 1993), for instance, slows down Hitchcock's film, stretching it out to 24 hours instead of its original 90-minute duration:

> *24-Hour Psycho* may represent an elegiac moment for the cinema, but it also marks a new dawn, the beginning of an 'expanded cinema', which will grow in possibility as electronic technologies are overtaken by digital ones. In this aesthetic juncture André Bazin's perception of the cinema takes on a new relevance as it is possible to watch the slow process of mutation as 'the image of things is also the image of their durations' and the process of 'change mummified' becomes a spectacle in its own right. (*Death* 103)

Mulvey's intervention cannot be denied: she effectively puts delay, suspense, death into the moving image, like poison into a "living" medium. Mulvey is especially important to this discussion because she uses an informed psychoanalytic approach to study not only cinema language and content but also the technical nature of the medium. Rather than see the digital era as a turning away from the origins of cinema and celluloid film's supposed relation to truth via its indexicality, Mulvey sees great deconstructive potential in new forms of digital technology to open the medium up to new scrutiny, allowing her to explore hidden dimension of cinema's past.[6] Furthermore, as an apparatus theorist, Mulvey gives us an insight into cinema revolving around death and stillness that helps us to deconstruct an opposition that has been so pervasive and taken for granted for the history of film: the fact that cinema is more aligned with movement at the expense of stillness and delay.

Uncanny feelings are aroused by confusion between the animate and the inanimate, most particularly again associated with death and the return of the dead. The photograph's suspension of time, its conflation of life and death, the animate and the inanimate, raises not superstition so much as a sense of disquiet that is aggravated rather than calmed by the photograph's mechanical, chemical and indifferent nature. Mulvey, commenting on Barthes' association between photography and death, emphasizes the dominance of the mechanical, of *techne*, which leaves little or no room in photography for human intervention in the form of art:

> Whatever the nature of the art of photography, that is to say, its intervention, its style, there is a point at which the photographic act is not an artistic act, a point at which it registers passively and this poignant, piercing passivity represents the opportunity of this reference to death; it seizes a reality that is there, that was there in an indissoluble now. In a word, one must choose between art and death. Barthes's concept of the *punctum* is also based on a separation between the eye of the photographer and the eye of the camera. A detail, probably unnoticed by the photographer, suddenly captures the viewer's attention and emotion. (*Death* 60–61)

Mulvey articulates a sort of Derridean dissemination for the new media age. Her analysis emphasizes the detail, death, and delay. On the nature of the uncanny in cinema, Mulvey writes,

> As stillness intrudes into movement, the image freezes into the 'stop of death', taking the aesthetics of cinema that leads back to pre-cinema, and to photographical and psychoanalytic theories. The blurred boundaries between the living and the non-living touch on unconscious anxieties that then circulate as fascination as well as fear in the cultures of the uncanny. (*Death* 32)

The stillness also does something a lot more tangible, that is conscious, revealing artificiality and *techne* at once, the *phainesthai*, and activates mourning.

While Eisenstein's montage assembled signs and put them in a system of classification, deconstruction slows down the medium, delaying final versions. Deconstruction, in short, reminds us cinema *is* photography. Montage can be used to alter temporal and spatial continuity. It can also be used to contrast stillness and motion which is the type closest to Derrida's conception of photography. Through montage filmmakers present ways of showing cinema's reliance on stillness even as most films privilege motion. Notable examples are found in Chris Marker and Jean-Luc Godard. By looking at slow motion as a form of montage we gain an awareness of the underlying technics of cinema's ghostly substance, and thus this new form of montage performs a certain deconstructive function beyond its basic semiotic one. The great theorist of realist cinema, Siegfried Kracauer, acknowledges slow motion's anti-natural effects. Describing *Desert Victory* (US, 1943), Kracauer writes, "racing legs shown in slow-motion do not just slow down but change in appearance and perform bizarre evolutions" (53). Mulvey argues that such unnatural, bizarre realities are the very stuff that underlies the medium.

In *Camera Lucida*, Barthes also sees a connection between photography and cinema. Barthes has a major revelation on photography precisely when watching Fellini's *Casanova* (Italy/US, 1976). He experiences a sense of pity when watching the Fellini automaton (116). It is at this point in the book that the death effect of photography joins up with cinema:

> I collected in a last thought the images which had 'pricked' me (since this is the action of the *punctum*), like that of the black woman with the gold necklace and the strapped pumps. In them, inescapably, I passed beyond the unreality of the thing represented, I entered crazily into the spectacle, into the image, taking into my arms what is dead, what is going to die, as Nietzsche did when, as Podach tells us, on January 3, 1889, he threw himself in tears on the neck of a beaten horse: gone mad for Pity's sake. (Barthes, *Camera* 116–117)

Garrett Stewart also tries to find a deathly connection between photography and cinema:

> What is dead about a corpse is not only its stasis but the sense of subtracted life it conveys, the sense of what has been evacuated from behind its eyes. Moving pictures no less than static ones are a visible function of nonpresence, a trace of the passed away. Such photographically based representation results in either a disembodied imprint on paper or spectral emanation from the imprinted celluloid in the projector. The immediate difference of stillness from motion in these two media may therefore serve in the end merely to specify deaths' relation to both. The difference, one might say, is between the cadaverous and the ghostly. (37)

In contradistinction to the written text or even painting, the *punctum* of photography, and now cinema, invites a kind of mourning that touches on madness. This gets back to Derrida's point: the *punctum* of all photography and film is that the thing will die. Thus, slow motion in Godard's *Every Man for Himself*, or *Slow Motion*, expands the meaning of the shot. Godard knows the technology will one day, pave the way for more manipulation. Godard's use of video in the 1970s reminds us of the possible ways of using this archiving machine for iterability. If Godard began his career by introducing the jump cut and thus transforming film continuity, in *Every Man For Himself* he tried to do the same, this time through an innovative use of slow motion.

A few scenes illustrate this point well. One is a domestic scene with all three main characters. Paul (Jacques Dutronc) and Denise (Nathalie Baye) sit at the kitchen table eating breakfast. Isabelle (Isabelle Huppert) enters the apartment and walks into the kitchen. Paul reads the title of a magazine article: "'100 Do-It-Yourself Ideas,' my God!" he exclaims. He closes the magazine and says to Denise, "I've got an idea." She responds, "You?" As he throws himself on top of her she yells, "Hey, what are you doing?" The film slows down to a crawl. There is the sound of dishes smashing and Gabriel Yared's music begins to dominate the soundtrack. They both fall to the floor. He has his arm wrapped around her neck like a snake. They tussle on the floor. Then, once Isabelle's presence is acknowledged, the film returns to regular motion photography. Isabelle says, "I called about the flat. What happened?" Paul tells her, "We can't seem to touch without bruising." Isabelle says, "You're crazy." Then Paul leaves and Isabelle smiles at Denise.

Godard explains his use of slow motion in this scene and the rest of the film on *The Dick Cavett Show* in 1980:

> If I did it at the normal speed it was not possible to see things or at least indicate a possibility, which is not completely reached here that there is something different to be seen. For example, they were fighting together but you had to indicate they were still in love together ... To slow it down just to have the time to look. To take your time to look at what you are doing, and then you discover that these movements ... It can be whether a jab or whether a caress. And then probably I was not capable enough of doing it completely. The shot is too long. Maybe there should be a change of angles and different timings. But I kept it that way because it was an indication. They want to love each other, but the only way they want to love each other, the only possibility is by touching themselves though jabs. So you indicate to the audience there is a possible that moves are changing ... So you use it ... It was only because I was working in the movies and the techniques in movies are very conservative. They don't want to link it with video. Or the video people don't want to be linked with movie people. And then I thought of it later. And not before the shooting. And that's why it's still awkward. It still looks a bit like a gadget. A gimmick like in a Sylvester Stalone movie. (*Every Man*)

When Godard talks about a better use of slow motion, he is referring to the first section of the film when Denise is biking through the Swiss countryside. Here, the slow motion allows her figure, the trees, the sky and road to "blend together." When Derrida writes in reference to cinema in "Force and Signification," he could almost be describing such innovative use of slow motion:

> [F]or as long as the metaphorical sense of the notion of structure is not acknowledged *as such*, that is to say interrogated and even destroyed as concerns its figurative quality so that the nonspatiality or original spatiality designated by it may be revived, one runs the risk, through a kind of sliding as unnoticed as it is *efficacious*, of confusing meaning

with its geometric, morphological, or, in the best of cases, cinematic model. One risks being interested in the figure itself to the detriment of the play going on within it metaphorically. (*Writing* 18)

Burchill locates the cinematic corollary of *différance* in Chris Marker's *La Jetée*. The film about a time traveller in post-apocalyptic Paris is composed nearly exclusively with still images. The question of the image is in fact the question of the film itself. The hero travels through time but cannot know with certainty if the images he experiences are real, dreams, or something other. Notably, the photo-montage contains a single motion picture shot. When the woman the man loves lies in bed on a lovely morning, a single shot captures her blinking. Burchill writes,

> It is precisely while the voice-over relates the man's questioning the mode of belief he credits to her existence, that the woman ... is suddenly imbued with movement ... [T]his is the only moment in the film composed not of a series of still photographs but of 'normal cinematic movement,' which, as such, entails that the images on the film reel not only succeed each other at the rate of twenty-four per second but that they differ between themselves. (176)

Burchill sees a clear parallel here with Derrida's explanation of spacing.

What if this moment of motion doesn't necessarily give us "life" or "motion" or "presence," as some critics have claimed, and indeed as the film sets up, but rather the shot gives us more of the death effect usually ascribed to photography and definitely not cinema? The blink is preceded by a series of impeccably timed dissolves—perceived like a slow motion shot—of her lying on the bed: "[T]he transition from filmed stasis to filmed kinesis is almost imperceptible" (Burchill 177). The series of dissolves gives us the sense of movement *before* "motion" actually happens. When the moment of "normal cinematic movement" arrives, we get a sense of relief. It is seen as "natural." The film can be summarized thus: cold, dead, time travel in photography. Love and life and presence in motion. The film seems to pit life and death against each other. Delay is seen as the antithesis of cinema. But even the moment of motion is now undeniably based on the photographic basis of the medium. We are never more aware of the stillness underlying the simulated motion. The film offers us a view of technics before naturalism.

La jetée leaves us with the sense that images indeed make up consciousness, including the unconscious. Visibility is equivalent with what is known, with what we, in a way, possess, as the hero possesses, obsesses, appropriates the women. Of course, Marker's inspiration from Hitchcock compounds this theme of obsession with the *image* of a woman. We don't respect visibility in the same way that we do invisibility. Spectrality includes an element of suspense, and thus, fear. The hero haunts the woman, thus, possessing her.

How is delay already anticipated in *Derrida*? On the *Derrida* DVD released by Zeitgeist Video in 2003, the deleted scenes and chapter access offer new ways of altering the order and repeating the film. While some features on the DVD like the commentary ostensibly put things in a more linear order than the actual film, others would in fact expand and throw us off narrative track and prevent clean conceptual framings. The haircut, too, makes us question the proper boundaries and obvious outtakes of Derrida. In a deleted scene called "Xerox," we are shown a series of repetitions and moments when Derrida checks his watch that reveals the slightly mechanical nature of his daily life.[7] Two other shots of Derrida's gaze toward the camera in *Derrida* are instructive. One is the "biographical" anecdotes sequence and the other is the final shot of Derrida sitting while the film crew work in the background—two shots echoing each other in their use of slow motion, delay, and the ghostly presence of meeting of the other's eyeline.

The Paris street shot only features Derrida looking straight at the camera once and none of the biographical details take predominance over another. The last shot grows more powerful as the filmmakers stand back and with a contemplative distance examine the gaze. Slow motion acts as an invitation to slow down and delay an image. But they occur precisely at moments when biographical information is being discussed. Maybe the only use of slow motion that isn't tied to a Derrida excerpt is the filmmaker's self-proclaimed amateurish voice-over is the "National Enquirer" shot of Derrida walking down the Paris street smoking a pipe. The shot is also notable because it presents as much biographical information as possible yet the image alternates between motion and stillness. This shot is also used on the DVD main menu with Ryuichi Sakamoto's icy music played over it.

The first one: What is Derrida's life based on? The second one: What was the trauma of his life? They both have to do with who his originary secret, the thing that can explain who he *is*. Both scenes can only give us a slowed down Derrida, caught in the technics of delay. Both times we may project but we always come up with an image of the other without the answers. The series of anecdotes offer various possible explanations and keys/cuts that will finally allow for comprehension: "His parents never read any of his books," "One side of his face is paralyzed for three weeks leaving his eye open continuously unblinking," "He fails his first entrance exam to the University," "He doesn't circumcise his sons greatly upsetting his Mother and Father," "He declines an offer from Marguerite Duras to play a part in one of her films" (Dick and Ziering Kofman 61). Later, the thriller-style shot of the California house puts us in the uncomfortable position of a voyeur doing the best job he possibly can. The film rushes back into stillness immediately after another of those "key" questions are asked: can we get any insight from the traumas of your life? This time, the stillness is due to Derrida's own very still body language. Nicholas Royle correctly asks just how long can this shot of Derrida's face, which includes his gaze at the camera lens, last (Dick and Ziering Kofman 20)? The enigmatic gaze and theatrical silence are emphasized in the final moments of the film. This slightly antagonistic gaze is one of presence yet its meaning remains almost completely out of reach. It goes far beyond a look that says, "Are you seriously asking me that?" What will be the key or password to Derrida? The film offers many possibilities, but mostly a sense that all the filmmakers could get was a photographic portrait, that is, a structure of absence and presence.

Slow motion proved a useful tool for Ziering who reads excerpts from Derrida's texts throughout the film. Ziering's voice-overs are moments of appropriation and *différance*. What does Derrida's philosophy mean in another's voice? What will it mean in the future, when others' speak it? Often these voice-over excerpts are read over images of a grey Paris under construction, a city that is changing, dying a little each day, and thus draws a rich parallel with what Derrida said about Athens: "Tomorrow, living Athens will be seen keeping and keeping an eye on, guarding and regarding, reflecting and reflecting on its deaths" (*Athens* 6). Pleshette DeArmitt explains the double movement of exappropriation in Derrida with reference to, among other things, *Derrida* and *Echographies of Television*. The Echo and Narcissus myth that Derrida meditates on in the documentary contains the principle dynamics of the decentred self:

> In speaking his language, in identifying with an interiorizing Narcissus, in sending his words back to him, Echo, Derrida contends, appropriates something of the other—his language or idiom—for herself … Echo appropriates something of Narcissus so that she may appropriate her*self* … Echo not only speaks in her *own name*, but also *declares her love*. ("Resonances of Echo" 97)

At the exact moment of counter-signing, we have a delayed image track that does many things simultaneously, including presenting the death effect via a city under transformation or a man getting his hair cut, proliferating *punctums*, and promoting blindness through concentrated slowness. Such technological inventiveness ensures the staging of the necessary futurity of spectrality, to paraphrase Gerhard Richter (*Copy* XXXVII). In a sense these moments create room for future singularity. The creation of the Marguerite ghost through repetition and slowing down proves to be the peculiar one. We see Derrida watching Marguerite leave the house immediately after the section on the Irvine archive. Had Derrida lived longer, how would he speak to *this* ghost? We do know that a certain aspect of the footage of him and Marguerite comes back to him in a spectral structure when he claims not to have remembered being asked the question about how he and Marguerite met.

Derrida also appears in slow motion when he is watching previously recorded footage of himself and Marguerite. The act of watching, deciphering is stretched throughout the film. A spectral life is one based on delay. When shown the footage of Marguerite and himself being asked about their first meeting, Derrida says,

> Yes, I don't remember at all the first time you asked me and Marguerite and how we first met. I don't remember this at all. I like that scene precisely because we don't say anything. We think the same thing, but we don't say it. I was moved by the scene, I liked it a lot. But I liked it precisely because we said nothing. We were about to say something but we remained on the edge of an impossible confidence.

Who is the ghost of Marguerite supposed to haunt? Derrida, Derrideans, philosophy itself? Is she just an anecdote even while featuring as a prominent ghost in his archive?

The final shot begins after he is asked if there have been any traumas in his life. "What possible secret will alter the archive in times to come?" What will be ash? What will be the key to Derrida? The film offers many possibilities. Both times we project but always come up with nothing. Nicholas Royle describes the scene thus:

> There is something especially strange and painful about the silent vigilance of this ending in which the camera lingers on the face of the star so long. 'So long?' This is the question Hamlet asks, incredulously, in response to Ophelia's telling him how long it is since his father died; but it also serves as the enigmatic epigraph to Derrida's essay on Shakespeare's play, an essay that specifically identifies mourning with the sense that 'the time is out of joint'... How long will this image last? (Dick and Ziering Kofman 20)

There is something especially attractive about this dichotomy of stillness and movement. With its ability to simply play out, there is no need to contextualize the moving image, no pressure to be haunted by anything that isn't making itself present. In the realm of presence that 24 frames per seconds seemingly affords, there is the temptation to let the subject be his or her own biographer in terms of what he or she says to be present. The binary of stillness and movement can even be seen in the most recent TV biography of Derrida, *Jacques Derrida, Le courage de la pensée* (dir. Linhart, 2014) which premiered on ARTE in France. There is the implication that Derrida's moving image is a species of political activism or televisual relevance and that the early photographs speak of secrecy and indeterminacy. Derrida, in voice-over, speaks of his early tumultuous days as a student at École normale supérieure, comparing their exam systems to the guillotine. A class photograph is shown where Derrida appears to be unhappy. This stillness of his early life does not make the history unfathomable, but the filmmakers still go to great lengths to explain these images through talking head interviews.

The documentary tries to fix the indeterminacy of his early, more photographed, life by incorporating many film and video excerpts in its second half. The motion picture excerpts nearly all imply a certain alertness to social issues and political position-taking, and therefore emphasize the present. Television interviews with Régris Debray on the Israeli-Palestine conflict and excerpts from *D'ailleurs, Derrida* on South African reconciliatory efforts position him as a public intellectual and strong televisual presence. Presence is even more emphasized in the Derrida excerpt where young female students introduce themselves and ask for his autograph. In the second half of the TV film, these clips are framed by Derrida's media availability and presence. News footage of Derrida arriving at the Paris train station after his imprisonment in Prague with many students and supporters gathered around him is punctuated by a freeze frame on Derrida's face after he is being asked questions by reporters. Back to stillness: the lack of availability and the closure of truth.

Under cinema's motion, is stillness: cinema's heightened presence is something it uses to its advantage. *Différance* enters the scene because it sees something uncanny within something that is already hidden. *Différance* promotes change and delay while spectrality lures us with its promises. By utilizing slow motion, repetition, and re-filming, films like *Derrida* tell us something about the conditions of representation. These strategies suggest the moment of filming or photographing—which is usually understood as a form of presence—is never simply done and over, never isolatable as an undivided present, but always conditional on the technics that representation—indeed all meaning—depends on.

Derrida would want us to note the technics of film, the elements that constitute its truth in the moment of reception.

Notes

1. Saghafi further clarifies, "In photography, the referential trait is split by a metonymic force that prevents the trait from ever being uniquely itself but also constitutes it in this process of self-detachment and splitting. This division (or spectrality, we may say) is what allows for the possibility of repetition and technical reproduction. Thus the 'unique death' and 'the instantaneous [*l'instantané*]' are always susceptible to metonymy" (97).
2. See Barthes' description of the portrait of William Casby (*Camera* 34).
3. In his writings on aesthetics, such as *Truth in Painting*, Derrida advocated an approach to ethics that goes against Kantian idealism. Ethics for Derrida is both universal and unknowable.
4. Importantly, Derrida's first attempt to explain deconstruction to Ziering in *Derrida* is punctuated by the example of the Rodney King video. Derrida addresses a classroom of students while he is being filmed from a camera in the corner of the room. In French, he says, "I want to explain the presence of and ask your permission for this film crew on my left. They'll be recording some images and I hope this occurs as imperceptibly as all the other recording devices we've become accustomed to. Recording devices, notably video or filmic ones, have been a topic of our seminar. On several occasions, we examined them in light of the example posed by the Rodney King verdict. This is a California film crew, by the way. In that case we posed the question: What happens to the testimonial archive when one takes into account that the classic definition of testimony excludes the intervention of recording devices? So as an experiment we'll see what it's like to work for a moment in the presence of these archiving machines."
5. Due to the nature of deconstructive analysis, it would seem appropriate to include material that could be considered extra-textual or paratextual, like DVD bonus materials, behind the scenes footage, deleted scenes, chapter selection, and interviews, in our analysis. Special features and chapter access have also influenced the way Mulvey reads cultural artefacts: "These extra-diegetic elements have broken through the barrier that has traditionally protected the diegetic world of narrative film and its linear structure … [A]s a DVD indexes a film into chapters, the heterogeneity of add-ons is taken a step further by non-linear access to its story … [T]hese new features also enhance understanding of the movies of the past, shifting them from pure entertainment into a quasi-museum-like status" (*Death* 27). I am receptive to this kind of material for its practicality, too.
6. Recently, Thomas Elsaesser has argued the transition from film—indexical photography—to the digital has resulted in a "crisis of representation" in film culture and studies (54–55). The "new wave" movements of European cinema, such as Italian neo-realism, and their articulation of national identities were suddenly replaced by the groundlessness of new media, digital cinema. Under this "crisis," the real and virtual are forced to coexist and find expression in "post-mortem" films, like Amenábar's *The Others* (2001). There is a sense, as Elsaesser acknowledges, the digital has played a fundamental role in articulating and constructing "our hyphenated and always already occupied identities" (61).
7. For a thorough analysis of the experimentalism of the deleted scenes specifically in *Derrida* see Sarah Dillon's *Deconstruction, Feminism, Film* (103–105).

Bibliography

Amenábar, Alejandro, dir. *The Others*. 2001. DVD. Alliance Atlantis, 2002.

Ariès, Philippe. *Western Attitudes toward Death: From the Middle Ages to the Present*. Trans. Patricia M. Ranum. Baltimore, MD: The John Hopkins University Press, 1974.

Barthes, Roland. *Camera Lucida: Reflections on Photography*. Trans. Richard Howard. York: Hill and Wang, 1981.

Baudry, Jean-Louis. "Ideological Effects of the Cinematographic Apparatus." *Narrative, Apparatus, Ideology: A Film Theory Reader*. Ed. Philip Rosen. New York: Columbia University Press, 1986.

Brunette, Peter, and David Wills. *Screen/Play: Derrida and Film Theory*. Princeton, NJ: Princeton University Press, 1989.

———, eds. *Deconstruction and the Visual Arts: Art, Media, Architecture*. Cambridge and New York: Cambridge University Press, 1994.

Burchill, Louise. "Derrida and the (Spectral) Scene of Cinema." *Film, Theory and Philosophy: The Key Thinkers*. Ed. Felicity Colman. Montréal: McGill-Queen's University Press, 2009.

Butler, Judith. "Endangered/Endangering: Schematic Racism and White Paranoia." *Reading Rodney King: Reading Urban Uprising*. Ed. Robert Gooding-Williams. New York: Routledge, 1993.

DeArmitt, Pleshette. "Resonances of Echo: A Derridean Allegory." *Mosaic* 42.2 (June 2009): 89–100.

Derrida, Jacques. *Writing and Difference*. Trans. Alan Bass. London: Routledge, 1978.

———. *Of Grammatology*. Trans. Gayatri Chakravorty Spivak. Baltimore and London: The Johns Hopkins University Press, 1997.

———. *The Work of Mourning*. Ed. Pascale-Anne Brault and Michael Naas. Chicago, IL: University of Chicago Press, 2001.

———. *Athens, Still Remains: The Photographs of Jean-François Bonhomme*. Trans. Pascale-Anne Brault and Michael Naas. New York: Fordham University Press, 2010a.

———. *Copy, Archive, Signature: A Conversation on Photography*. Trans. Jeff Fort. Stanford, CA: Stanford University Press, 2010b.

Derrida, Jacques, and Marie-François Plissart. *Right of Inspection*. Trans. David Wills. New York: Monacelli Press, 1998.

Dick, Kirby, and Amy Ziering Kofman, dirs. *Derrida*. 2002. DVD. Zeitgeist Video, 2003.

———, eds. *Derrida: Screenplay and Essays on the Film Derrida*. Manchester: Manchester University Press, 2005.

Dillon, Sarah. *Deconstruction, Feminism, Film*. Edinburgh: Edinburgh University Press, 2018.

Elsaesser, Thomas. "Real Location, Fantasy Space, Performative Place: Double Occupancy and Mutual Interference in European Cinema." *European Film Theory*. Ed. Temenuga Trifonova. New York and London: Routledge, 2009.

Godard, Jean-Luc. *Every Man for Himself*. 1980. Blu-ray. The Criterion Collection, 2015.

Hitchcock, Alfred, dir. *Psycho*. 1960. DVD. Universal Home Video, 1998.

Kracauer, Siegfried. *Theory of Film: The Redemption of Physical Reality*. Oxford: Oxford University Press, 1960.

Linhart, Virginie, dir. *Jacques Derrida, Le courage de la pensée*. 2014. ARTE.

Marker, Chris, dir. *La jetée/Sans soleil*. 1983. DVD. The Criterion Collection, 2007.

Mulvey, Laura. *Death 24x a Second: Stillness and the Moving Image*. London: Reaktion Books, 2006.

Naas, Michael. "When It All Suddenly Clicked: Deconstruction after Psychoanalysis after Photography." *Mosaic* 44/3 (September 2011): 81–98.

Rosen, Philip, ed. *Narrative, Apparatus, Ideology: A Film Theory Reader*. New York: Columbia University Press, 1986.

Saghafi, Kas. *Apparitions—Of Derrida's Other*. New York: Fordham University Press, 2010.

Stewart, Garrett. *Between Film and Screen: Modernism's Photo Synthesis*. Chicago, IL: University of Chicago Press, 1999.

Tarkovsky, Andrei, dir. *The Mirror*. 1974. DVD. Kino Video, 2000.

CHAPTER THREE

2nd *Séance*: The Dead Sound Off: Mourning Others in *Ghost Dance*

Ghost Dance, from 1983, stages the work of mourning on multiple fronts, including radical uses of sound and image. The unhinged voices proliferating throughout never allow the total incorporation of the other. What we get instead are traces of machinic recordings of the other that disseminate and re-emerge unexpectedly. *Ghost Dance* focuses on a young woman who confronts and studies the ghosts of the postmodern city and society. The film was shot in Paris and London, and in the London scenes derelict, industrial locations are used to signal among other things the ghosts of a certain urban working-class culture. Derrida is featured throughout to explain cinema's ghostly nature as well as to offer further insights on mourning and other laws that render us blind, like in his retelling of his Kafkaesque imprisonment in Prague the previous year or his voice-over monologue on mourning over derelict walls and photos of communards. As the title suggests, multiple scenes in *Ghost Dance* carry a ghostly quality, emphasizing the mediated presence of others, including Pascale breaking up with a lover via a tape recorder, photographic reminders of the Paris commune, Derrida meeting someone spontaneously over the telephone, a character who sleeps under a poster of Marx's tombstone, voices in Pascale's head as she types her dissertation, and stills from the film thrown into the sea at the end.

In the larger frame of Derrida's overall career, the making of *Ghost Dance* was an important event for the conjuring of ghosts. The film is a direct influence on

Specters of Marx. My reading of *Ghost Dance* will attempt to synthesize the film with two "long" explanations of spectrality found in *Specters* and *Echographies of Television.* Why does Derrida bring up the topic of visibility and telecommunications in *Specters* only to drop it quickly and not offer concrete examples? We cannot conceive of spectrality without taking into consideration out of jointness *and* blindness *and* inheritance *and* mourning—four key themes are articulated perhaps most aptly because of the cinematic apparatus and explored in these experimental films.

McMullen made *Ghost Dance* (West Germany/UK, 1983) on a shoestring budget after a series of performance pieces. *Zina* (UK, 1985) was his first film with a large budget, financed by television and commercial film companies. His films have mixed revolutionary politics and formal experimentation (Leahy 138). *Ghost Dance* engages with the ethico-political dimension of spectrality and deconstruction in sometimes eccentric and humorous ways. The film marks Derrida's willingness to appear in the media. Many things coincide at roughly this same time. It is the beginning of the "ethical turn," wherein spectrality becomes a key concern. The antinomies of political haunting and inheritance are closely investigated in McMullen's 1985 follow-up *Zina*—a fictionalization of Trotsky's time in exile as recounted by his daughter Zina. McMullen's avant-garde films remain an eccentric and imaginative exploration of 20th century haunting. *Ghost Dance* introduces the idea of the philosopher as a possessed entity through mourning, something *Zina,* through its depiction of the communication of historical revolutionaries, extends to include public intellectuals more generally. Although they have rarely been discussed, *Ghost Dance* and *Zina* open up a whole constellation of ideas related to intellectual subjectivities, spectrality, and revolutionary politics pre-1989, pre-*Specters of Marx.* The themes of teletechnology and neo-liberalism explored in the films are well-suited to the structure of spectrality and no doubt feed into it.

Ghost Dance engages with Derridean philosophy in the context of avant-garde film aesthetics. Derrida refers to *Ghost Dance* multiple times in later writings and interviews when discussing the experience of being photographed, and working with Pascale Ogier, the French actress who passed away shortly after making the film. The film in many ways sets the stage for the theme of spectrality in Derrida's later writing (e.g. *Specters of Marx*) as well as engages Derrida's philosophy in fascinating and decidedly experimental ways. In *Specters of Marx* (1993), a study of the ways Marxism still haunts post-1989 world culture, Derrida defines spectrality as a non-present inheritance that regards you, but that is temporally out of joint. McMullen's *Zina,* a narrative film about Trotsky's time in exile as recounted by his daughter Zina to a Berlin psychoanalyst. "My father isn't blind … He sees everything," Zina says during one of her sessions. As seen through a character that both haunts and is haunted by revolution, the film challenges the binaries between exile and home, speech and writing, presence and absence through experimental forms of montage and mise-en-scène, all while capturing the politics and psychology of inheritance during the period leading up to the Second World War.

In *Ghost Dance* and *Zina*, the inheritance always comes from another time and through media (letters, photography, radio, or oral stories). *Zina*, a narrative film about Trotsky's time in exile as recounted by his daughter Zina Bronstein (Domiziana Giordano) to a Berlin psychoanalyst (Ian McKellen) who keeps a meticulous record of her sessions, explores the antinomies of political inheritance. Characters communicate through letter writing. A letter written by Zina that Trotsky sent to her psychologist Kronfeld who sees it as Trotsky's attempt to enter the analytic space, is the subject of a scene that illustrates deconstruction's blurring of presence and non-presence. The protagonist's psychologist Kronfeld (Ian McKellen) re-reads Zina's letter. The film then cuts to Trotsky in exile, being read Zina's letter by his assistant. As the letter is read, the camera starts to pan and shows a huge hole in the wall of the building. The camera pans left, goes outside, passes a cliff, and then Zina is there in person speaking with Trotsky, who has suddenly switched places. Zina forcefully warns him about the encroaching threat of fascism. The camera then repeats the same motion backwards. The assistant finishes reading the letter to Trotsky. The film cuts back to Kronfeld reading the letter. The shot blurs divisions, between the written and oral, exile and non-exile, original and copy. The scene is about rereading without an origin.

The scene blurs distinctions in a similar way that Derrida sought to deconstruct Plato's notion of writing:

> Plato thinks of writing, and tries to comprehend it, to dominate it, on the basis of *opposition* as such. In order for these contrary values (good/evil, true/false, essence/appearance, inside/outside, etc.) to be in opposition, each of the terms must be simply *external* to the other, which means that one of these oppositions (the opposition between inside and outside) must already be accredited as the matrix of all possible opposition. (*Dissemination* 103)

Zina and Trotsky who are *both* in exile are at times credited with witnessing the encroachment of fascism in Germany. She over-identifies with Trotsky, declaring at one point that she is selfless, and is shocked when Trotsky suddenly appears. At the end, caught in a hospital under attack in 1942 Stalingrad, Kronfeld asks a nurse to pass on Zina's sessions tapes to "People in the future." He asks the assistant to memorize these lines: "In the nine years since Zina's suicide, Trotsky's prophecy has come about. We don't know what we take in on an unconscious level. What we internalize, and how these things can reemerge."

Zina presents a series of mediations around the theme of exile, family, and political engagement. The first shot is of Zina's therapist explaining how she is shielded from her biographical origins. After a period of exile in which Zina became even more alienated from Trotsky, who is seen recording his political ideas into a phonograph, she moves to Berlin and, at the request of her father, begins therapy. Kronfeld also records everything Zina says about her family, turning a family drama into a spectral medium that can ostensibly last generations. Does the film display a nostalgic hunger for origins, or does it suggest the Trotsky family will produce spectral relationships? McMullen advocates a position of mid-mourning as he shows how the key anti-fascist message is successfully carried on through time.

Ghost Dance follows Pascale (Pascale Ogier), a young student who meets various people in both real and surreal situations all having to do with the existence of ghosts. The recording devices that proliferate in the films place everything at a potential remove, creating an uncanny experience even from the most natural-seeming scenes. In the first half hour, Derrida plays "Philosopher" and his voice-over is heard two more times later in the film. What hasn't been noted as much are the ways *Ghost Dance* sets the stage for the theme of spectrality in Derrida's later writing, especially *Specters of Marx*. I suggest that it is in fact Derrida's experience with filmmaking, being photographed and re-watching the film, and *Ghost Dance* in particular that allows him to elaborate certain "cinematic" aspects of spectrality in *Specters of Marx*.

Heritage and the spectre share a close relationship. Hamlet's ghost speaks of justice, law, the paternal connection that is assured, but there is no inheritance without this spectral dimension that speaks to you directly, that requires an answer from you (Derrida, *Specters* 18). Derrida explains the spectral inheritance in terms of an anachronism. All anachronisms are ghosts. How is inheritance heterogeneous? Derrida stresses: "If the readability of a legacy were given, natural, transparent, univocal, if it did not call for and at the same time defy interpretation, we would never have anything to inherit from it" (*Specters* 18). The ghost is never merely seen yet there is connection with its singularity. Inheritance concerns you, but isn't seen. While it isn't seen directly, one way to read spectres is in the media by which they are transmitted and carried. What we inherit first passes through technology, given its out of joint quality. In *Ghost Dance*, for instance, the inheritance always comes from another time and through technology, whether photography, radio, or folklore.

At one point, in *Ghost Dance*, the protagonists dance in their apartment dressed in tribal wear. The film then dissolves to the images of the dead of the 1871 French commune. It is at this highly eccentric point that Derrida returns. This time, he is heard, but not seen. Over photographs of dead revolutionaries on the decaying walls we get the following lesson in ghosts, this "ghost science." Via voice-over, Derrida develops an idea from Abraham and Torok:

> Freud! We were talking about the ghost of Freud. You know, ghosts don't just appear. They come back. In French we talk of them "returning." Now that presupposes a memory of the past that has never taken the form of the present. But I've been intrigued by a particular theory which some psychoanalyst friends of mine—Nicolas Abraham, who's now dead, and Maria Torok—developed from Freud. Their theory of ghosts is based on a theory of mourning. In normal mourning, Freud says one internalizes the dead. One takes the dead into oneself … and assimilates them. This internalization is an idealization. It accepts the dead. Whereas in mourning which doesn't develop naturally, that is to say, in mourning that goes wrong, there is no true internalization.

He continues to develop this idea of post-structuralist psychoanalysis by claiming the other *in us* can, in fact, *speak* in our place. In film, images haunt, but the voice of the philosopher is especially haunting.[1] Film typically captures voice and speech in a synchronous now that binds time to space. But the voice is *already* out of joint. Why does his voice replace his image? Is it uncannier because of the voice's immediacy? John Durham Peters argues media that record the voice are experienced as uncanny due to their relatively recent development (160).

Like all films, *Ghost Dance* is out of joint, with its time and space. Its disjointed soundtrack constantly forces us to encounter the other in a ghostly, disembodied fashion, perhaps more than most films. The film begins with Pascale recording herself on a tape recorder, and then replaying it. She later tells a professor she runs into that she records his lectures and therefore never has to attend his classes: "I like juxtapositions. So I like to play it anyplace, like in bars, in the bath, in the subway. And you should be pleased because I've made you a kind of God. You're in all places at all times." The photographs of dead commune revolutionaries, superimposed voice-overs, and Derrida's voice-over over a shot of waves work together to give the sense of disharmony. Since the sound- and image-tracks have been created at different, unknown times, there is no natural order.

This unsettling, out of place voice has a strong parallel with how the phantom operates in the psyche. Timothy Secret explains the phantom has its own secret force, a truly unintentional return of an inherited crypt: "A phantom occurs with the *mise en abyme* structure of the incorporation of a psychic topography that is itself already fractured by a crypt with its own secret" (168). The voice that returns to the psychic apparatus seeks justice in the form of a "material novelty":

> That I experience myself as addressing the dead *themselves* in eulogy, troubled by a desire to do justice to *them*, would no longer be a mere fiction or absurdity, even if the real persistence of the dead within the psyche remains rooted as an act of fantasy. (Secret 169)

The language of the crypt that Secret proposes is at heart based on discontinuity, where one thing can exist in another without smooth incorporation or even synthesis in a dialectical sense. As such, film works a whole lot like the psychic apparatus that creates a *mise en abyme* composition of mixed media and discontinuous traces.

In *Recording Reality, Desiring the Real*, Elizabeth Cowie defines time, documentary time, and duration. How to distinguish "real time" from a presentation of liveness? Cowie draws on Derrida to show how history is created in the traces, anterior to the live event, forcing us to question the supposed spontaneity of the live event. Television is never simply live. What is left out of the event of writing: the ideal signified, the fully present. Since this is unobtainable, the whole discourse on spectrality enters the scene as what haunts the trace. The subject isn't accessible; never not meant for *re*broadcast. Cowie stresses how telecommunications are used to reproduce liveness, simultaneity, and contemporaneity. We forget there is a writing presentation, a form to communication. Emergencies are often experienced through reproductive technologies. Cowie then offers examples of uncanny voices of 9/11 victims from phone calls (155). These traces of the departed have indeed survived. The disembodied voice's tactility is somehow uncannier than the image because the image is too often used as a form of direct access, contemporaneity.

In "The Voice in the Cinema: The Articulation of Body and Space," Mary Ann Doane argues that film is constructed to offer presence out of disparate elements. Sound in film is usually anchored to the image, the more overt signifier. "There is always something uncanny about a voice which emanates from a source outside the frame," (368) writes Doane. While these elements are actually all disembodied, narrative film sutures them together and thus suppresses their disembodied quality. Doane continues,

> The aural illusion of position constructed by the approximation of sound perspective and by techniques which spatialize the voice and endow it with 'presence' guarantees the singularity and stability of a point of audition, thus holding at bay the potential trauma of dispersal, dismemberment, difference. (371–372)

Voice is important in mourning and in Derrida. In *Specters*, he writes,

> To feel ourselves seen by a look which it will always be impossible to cross, that is the visor effect on the basis of which we inherit from the law. Since we do not see the one who sees us, and who makes the law, who delivers the injunction (which is, moreover, a contradictory injunction), since we do not see the one who orders 'swear' we cannot identify it in all certainty, we must fall back on its voice. (7)

Unlike the spirit or phantom of ideology, spectrality still keeps some *relation* to the body—it suggests "the tangible intangibility of a proper body without flesh, but always some*one* as some*one* other" (Saghafi 54).

The voice in *Ghost Dance* and *Zina* creates an uncanny disembodied experience of the subject. The long shot in *Zina* works in a way to constantly readjust our interpretation of the events. In terms of seeing, Zina's voice-off immediately puts her in mind then once we see her, we can no longer see the image we had of her in our mind. Trotsky's silence serves to hide his co-authorship of the letter's warnings. No stage of full presence. At one point, Trotsky is heard in mono sound when Hitler's voice in booming stereo interrupts him. McMullen wanted to suggest that Trotsky is just one voice that gets drowned out, giving it a ghostly status whereas Hitler's recorded voice may now re-emerge at any time, giving fascism a future unknowable audience.

Ghost Dance's rich soundtrack, comprised of voice-over, voice-off, dialogue, haunting music, discordant sound effects overlap and combine in ways that always emphasizes out of jointness. George (Robbie Coltrane) angers the protagonists because of his incessant drum-playing while listening to the radio weather forecast. Derrida's voice-overs on mourning and Kafka in a sense haunt every other moment of the film. This adestination gives communication its spectral quality, always implying a more to come. In a 1986 France Culture radio interview on the program *Le Bon plaisir*, McMullen explains his interest in the philosopher:

> Derrida for me is inspirational. His texts are extremely difficult and I don't necessarily read them cover to cover. But I read them, I move in and out of them, and carry certain notions and ideas around. And some of those ideas, I suppose, I re-articulate them and attempt to put some of them in dramatic form. That's how the theory enters the film ...[*Ghost Dance*] begins with the statement long before language, in a past without form, they began to appear in the darkness of night. What this hints at: before language as a social phenomena and before language in personal development terms, already text is being established ... The film is not a linear narrative. It is an accumulative narrative. In other words, it has five or six sections which overlay each other. And meaning jumps between these levels, underlaying sections. In that sense, I think that maybe even the form that Derrida writes in presents itself to some extent within the film. Because I think sometimes my impression of reading Derrida is that the concepts become defined by reading a number of sections because to some considerable extent really concepts are always undefinable. They become lost in language. ("Le Bon plaisir")

Mourning can be conceived as being possessed by voices you didn't know you internalized. And the voices in the film serve this suspense and dispersion effect. Derrida's influence on McMullen is certainly felt in the film, but what of McMullen's films has Derrida inherited?

Characters inhabited by other characters is a common theme in *Ghost Dance* and *Zina*. McMullen explains,

> I was very aware of the notion of registration. You take one level or registration which reveals the next which reveals the next, and so on. Like *The Arabian Nights*—inside each story is the beginning of the next. Like a maze: you can reassess your own starting point, or you can muse on the texture of the narrative strands. *Ghost Dance* hints at something I'm interested in, which is that when a character speaks it is actually a chorus of characters. In other words, the incorporated splinters of others channel that speech. Zina speaks not only from her father's position, but in the end from classical myth. She's carrying inside her the ghosts of many that have gone. The struggle for me is to get rid of the preconceptions that range in the psyche. (Leahy 139)

Both image and voice produce new interior ghosts. *Ghost Dance* speaks of generations going back to the seashore. Generations, and inheritance frame the whole. Or as Derrida puts it in *Specters*, "One never inherits without coming to terms with [*s'expliquer avec*] some specter, and therefore with more than one specter. With the fault but also the injunction of *more than one*" (24). Ogier records her breakup message: "Fuck you. I'm sick of it. I'm selling everything. I'm off. Don't try to find me. As far as I'm concerned, you're a ghost." She plays the message back to herself immediately after recording it and leaves the apartment. This is a promise to whoever lives there, to whoever inhabits the recording's time-space. Or could it be a message to herself? After all, the character is represented by two actresses after this scene. It is at the point of the playback of a recording machine that she is split in two. The message also reappears on the soundtrack right before Derrida's introduction: "Fuck you. I'm sick of it ... I'm off." Then we first see Derrida sitting in a café bar.

Derrida draws a parallel between his texts and the arts and emphasizes the polyvocality of his writing:

> [W]hat they have in the final analysis that is most analogous to spatial, architectural, and theatrical works is their acoustics and their voices. I have written many texts with several voices, and in them the spacing is visible. There are several people speaking, and this necessarily implies a dispersions of voices, of tones that space themselves, that automatically spatialize themselves ... People's reactions, their libidinal investments, positive or negative, their rejection or hatred, can probably be best explained in terms of tone and voice more than in terms of the content of what I actually say. (Brunette and Wills, *Deconstruction* 22)

Space is an obvious element of cinema, but voice doesn't get the attention it deserves, perhaps because it seems secondary to film's visual basis—temporalizing voice literally came after the spatializing visual. He defines beauty in art as that which we cannot consume, like the voice of the other:

> Beauty is something that awakens my desire by saying 'you will not consume me.' It is a joyful work of mourning, although neither work nor mourning ... There is a voice

that says that that can happen only with you, but it happens without you. That is beauty; it's sad, mourning. (Brunette and Wills, *Deconstruction* 23)

In *Ghost Dance*, Derrida says he is possessed by at least three ghosts: Freud, Kafka, and Marx. The Freudian ghost appears explicitly in the monologue reproduced above. In the film, Derrida performs as a ghost and says, "L'avenir est aux fantômes," the same promise made by Marx and Engels. As in *Specters of Marx*, there must be a promise. Derrida's promise was re-articulated when he wrote *Specters*. This forces us to ask what happens to a promise when it is repeated? Does it inaugurate a genre? Derrida spent one day on the set of *Ghost Dance*, and according to McMullen, the idea of being in something small and experimental appealed to him. McMullen had read some of Derrida's work, which would presumably have been the early 1960s books. In *Specters*, Derrida argues if we didn't have to talk with ghosts, we wouldn't be responsible for anything. Spectres allow us to make a choice, because every spectre is a kind of promise. Inheriting a responsibility is like mourning something over one's entire life. Moreover, Derrida's cameo is very Godardian. McMullen interviews Derrida very much the same way Godard interviews Brice Parain in *Vivre sa vie* (1962) and Francis Jeanson in *La chinoise* (1967): he asks a real life intellectual to speak with a fictional character. The scene is haunted by Godard, suggesting just how much film depends on iterability. The status of the cameo is supplementary in most cases; it functions as a moment apart, condensing all character history and motivation and commenting on the whole.

In his monologue, Derrida says,

And I believe that modern developments in technology and telecommunication instead of diminishing the realm of ghosts as does any scientific or technical thought is leaving behind the age of ghosts, as part of the feudal age with its somewhat primitive technology as a certain perinatal age. Whereas I believe that ghosts are part of the future. And that the modern technology of images, like cinematography and telecommunication, enhances the power of ghosts and their ability to haunt us. In fact, it's because I wished to tempt the ghosts out that I agreed to appear in a film.

Kittler opens *Gramophone, Film, Typewriter* with a meditation on ghosts in media, observing,

Photo albums establish a realm of the dead infinitely more precise than Balzac's competing literary enterprise, the *Comédie humaine*, could ever hope to create ... [P]hotographic plates—even and especially those taken with the camera shutter closed—furnished reproductions of ghosts or specters, whose black-and-white fuzziness only served to underscore the promise of resemblance. (11–12)

Although Kittler advocates "scientific" media studies that analyze "material communicative events," he is cognizant of the unavoidable spectral dimension of media. He adds,

> The realm of the dead is as extensive as the storage and transmission capabilities of a given culture ... If gravestones stood as symbols at the beginning of culture itself, our media technology can retrieve all gods ... In our mediascape, immortals have come to exist again. (13)

Pascale declares she is a student of ghosts: "I studied with Jacques Derrida. But he couldn't teach me everything. Because there are things that a man can't teach a woman." Pascale has one flashback memory in the film: the time she visited the Commune memorial in Paris. Is this her first encounter with the ghost? Is this the moment when her identity was first divided? The film ends with McMullen stating, "They see an image of the struggle with their own persona. They'll be left with that." The film returns us to the seashore. Images from the film are now partly buried in a muddy wall near the shore. Is mourning successful or not? This seems to be a decisive burial, the kind Freud argued for. Of course, all the characters are dead now, including Ogier, Derrida, Pinon, and Coltrane, dead, because photographed. But the image of the ocean doesn't leave us with a decisive burial. Back and forth, Fort:Da, the wave functions as a metaphor for mid-mourning. At the end of *every* film we mourn, throw images of characters into an ocean. Sometimes mourning is successful and we don't remember, but often today we see them again, they return as *revenants*, as Ogier would. The ocean, too, is spectral.

There are three ways that the character George represents the anti-Derridean perspective of sorts. As character, George moves into the narrative slowly, just as Derrida is on his way out. Is he another part of Pascale's psyche as we have been led to believe with Marianne? Or is he the "real" real character that seems to disrupt the film's dreamlike quality? How is George the counter voice to Derrida's, and why does it matter? First, George's improvisational jazz routine suggests he is an earthy guy, truly living in the present, like the exemplary liberal subject. The weather forecast connects his media consumption with his world-view and embrace of all things actual or real. In spite of the other characters' protests, George plays the drums incessantly to accompany the weather report, suggesting that his behaviour is pathological. His desire to repeat the act but never admitting anything is wrong turns it into a fetish.

Second, George thinks anything that is out of joint, old, different, in a word, other, is suspect. He makes fun of Pascale's thesis when a page gets jammed in the printer where he works—a scene that doesn't really make narrative sense unless George is a part of Pascale or this is her dream/nightmare. George seemingly equates the faulty machinery with a problem with Pascale's thought: "It's no wonder it gets jammed with this stuff in it. Thought you said this was a thesis?" "It is, but I need to write as word comes," Pascale explains. "Seems like pretty heavy to me. I'll maybe run myself off a copy and read it later. You must be a right nutcase to write this stuff. Hey, Jim, have you seen this? I, told you, it always gets jammed with filth in it. Same every time," George says. The scene ends with George laughing derisively at Pascale. "Why don't you just get your thesis and stick it up your bum!" Overseeing the smooth functioning of the Kodak printers, George brings to mind major telecoms that don't tolerate history or difference in their information flows. Pascale's thesis on ghosts literally breaks down the machinery of mediation.

The final way George represents an extreme version of the neoliberal subject is in the way he thinks he will achieve happiness in the end. After being rebuffed by Pascale and Marianne, he decides to get a shave, ponders a makeover, and decides to buy a suit. "I'd like to change my bone structure, but there's nothing I can do about that. I wish I could change my skin, but that would be too expensive." George believes happiness is achieved through physical beauty and self-improvement. George is the only character who explicitly forces himself upon another in a film about ghosts and ancient myths. He is a character that doesn't know the past or history and he is shied away when the conversation turns to dark sexual matters. George imposes himself on the protagonists because he possesses no understanding of anything outside of the present. George chases instant gratification while Derrida becomes a voice speaking to us ever more faintly from the past.

Haunted, haunting, Derrida also improvises but draws attention to the fact that he is already under the gaze of at least three: Freud, Kafka, and Marx. These three, this set, for Derrida, speaks of spectrality. Freud's uncanny and the Kafkaesque are perhaps more understandable as cinematic ghosts, but how does Marx work in this case? In his improvised comments, Derrida says he is haunted by Ogier, too. If we cannot be haunted by Kafka, Freud, and Marx, as Derrida is, then we are at least haunted by Derrida, who is haunted by Ogier, another possible point of shared haunting. In fact, it is alterity itself, that stand-in within this structure of spectrality. This is Saghafi's greater point in *Apparitions* when he writes on the connection between Ogier and Marx: "Derrida argues we must think the possibility of welcome or hospitality in conjunction with a thinking of the face" (35). The face of the other can in fact be monstrous—we are not called upon only to accept the human qualities of the other, but "other other" qualities, too. Drawing on Levinas, the God-Other pair is brought together within spectrality, according to Saghafi:

> In *Specters of Marx*, Derrida terms this asymmetrical relation in which we are unable to see what regards us "the *visor effect*," and underscores its significance, the "spectral asymmetry" of a gaze that cannot be returned, by stating that "*it will be presupposed by everything we advance on the subject of the specter in general*, in Marx and elsewhere." (53)

The other always has the accent of the ghost because of the way the visor effect presents itself as inheritance. Saghafi stresses, "This obedience, 'an essentially blind submission to his secret,' is 'a first obedience to the injunction,' the obedience conditioning all others to come" (54).

Already within presence, there is absence or rather the haunting of another image and voice. To Derrida, his image is not that of "Jacques Derrida," the philosopher type objectified, but of the other haunted by Kafka, Freud, and Marx. Being haunted by the otherness within himself, Derrida questions whether what we even get with the image is not always already spectral. The image, like the televised one, feigns presence in the form of liveness. Telecommunication seems to disseminate images that reflect the world as it is. Yet even in the most innocent form of the present, ghosts proliferate.

In 1984 and 1985, Derrida worked on his seminar "Le fantôme de l'autre" wherein he used the notion of the phantom in its political ideological sense of cultural nationalism to, among other things, deconstruct a text by Adorno wherein the author pitted a vulgar republican German nationalism against a "linguistic-philosophical" one. But spectrality gets perhaps first articulated and explored by Derrida in *Ghost Dance*. Derrida begins to explore the various forms of spectrality after his Prague imprisonment and his first step into fiction filmmaking. Indeed by the time of *Specters of Marx*, spectrality is refined to a point that necessarily incorporates visual culture and teletechnology. While Derrida doesn't refer to *Ghost Dance* in *Specters*, the book is full of cinematic concepts—it is "of the visible, but of the invisible visible, it is the visibility of a body which is not present in flesh and blood. It resists the intuition to which it presents itself, it is not *tangible*" (Derrida and Stiegler 115). While it's not surprising that cinema would be behind Derrida's main thesis on spectrality, it is perhaps worth noting Derrida's seeming avoidance of broaching film in his own writings. Both works speak to each other, as the film leaves things out that the movie takes up and vice versa. Could Pascale Ogier be the scholar of ghosts that Derrida calls for in *Specters*? Or is the Derrida of *Ghost Dance* the scholar he later conjures up in *Specters*? He doesn't mention *Ghost Dance* in *Specters*, but in the companion piece to *Specters*, *Echographies of Television*, a book that is devoted to cinematic technologies, he reflects at length on the experience of being filmed and what he calls the "night light" of video. But taken together, the film and book illuminate several key themes related to deconstruction: trace, spectrality, mourning, time, alterity, and responsibility.

In *Specters*, Derrida writes,

> The specter … is the *frequency* of a certain visibility. But the visibility of the invisible. And visibility, by its essence, is not seen, which is why it remains *epekeina tes ousias*, beyond the phenomenon or beyond being. The specter is also, among other

things, what one imagines, what one thinks one sees and which one projects—on an imaginary screen where there is nothing to see. Not even the screen sometimes, and a screen always has, at bottom, in the bottom or background that it is, a structure of disappearing apparition …[V]isible-invisible, the specter first of all sees *us*. From the other side of the eye, *visor effect*, it looks at us even before we see it or even before we see period. We feel ourselves observed, sometimes under surveillance by it even before any apparition. (125)

In *Ghost Dance* and *Zina*, spectrality is conceived as a suspension where the referent gets further away while at the same time the spectre's promise gets stronger. "In the virtual space of all the tele-technosciences, in the general dis-location to which our time is destined—as are from now on the places of lovers, families, nations— the messianic trembles on the edge of this event itself," (*Specters* 212–213) Derrida warns. Whatever concerns virtuality, the spectre, blindness, is absolutely key to these films and relevant to the collaborations and processes of making these films. Derrida conceives of a truly phantom, immaterial screen in the future:

All phantasms are projected onto the screen of this ghost (that is, on something absent, for the screen itself is phantomatic, as in the television of the future which will have no 'screenic' support and will project its images—sometimes synthetic images—directly on the eye, like the sound of the telephone deep in the ear). (*Specters* 123)

Echographies of Television is based on an interview that begins with the artifactual, and how television, through various mechanisms, creates "liveness," the effects that go toward facts based on technics. In "Spectrographies," Derrida recounts this very personal experience of filming the scene with Pascale Ogier, and then encountering her ghost, again, years later and after her death. Her answer to the question, which they rehearsed and repeated multiple times during production, of whether or not she believes in ghosts, "Yes, now I do, yes," almost makes more sense years later, amongst students in Texas. Derrida then develops an idea of law and the performative and how the spectrality means a right of inspection over you. It is the ring of these words—her voice in time—that returns and speaks to Derrida—a seeing voice—years later. We are free only if the other grants us this freedom. Being regarded can be both good and bad. This is not a pessimistic view or something to bemoan. He writes zestfully, "[M]y freedom springs from the condition of this responsibility which is born of heteronomy in the eyes of the other, in the other's sight. This gaze is spectrality itself" (Derrida and Stiegler 122).

The brief anecdote about the Texas screening is revealing on a number of fronts. Within the film, Derrida is playing the part of a professor teaching a student his theory of ghosts. Similarly, he is also within the moment of instruction when he screens *Ghost Dance* to students in Texas and encounters Ogier's gaze once again: "[A]s she *appears* on the large screen of an auditorium in Texas, he claims that hers is no simple look but a regard that remains asymmetrical" (Saghafi 55). In a social context where American cinema is correctly perceived as being dominant and where American stars occupy an unprecedented position of social and psychological influence on film audiences, Derrida shows these American students the spectres of the French philosopher and the French actress in a British film backed by German producers. "Içi le fantôme c'est moi!" he exclaims in the film, rightly suggesting the one filmed gets to be the ghost, as if we each take turns, film by film, in being the ghostly presence. By screening the film within the moment of instruction, Derrida stages his own inheritance as ghostly other for the American students.

Commenting on the material component of picture-taking, the way that the camera captures the lit subject, Derrida notes,

> This flow of light which captures or possesses me, invests me, or envelops me is not a ray of light, but the source of a possible view: from the point of view of the other. If the 'reality effect' is ineluctable, it is not simply because there is something real that is undecomposable, or not synthesizable, some 'thing' that was there. It is because there is something other that watches or concerns me. This Thing is the other insofar as it was already there—before me—ahead of me, beating me to it, I who am before it, I who am because of it, owing to it. (Derrida and Stiegler 123)

I am always in a position of inheriting the other. The spectre of death is never seen in the material flesh. The spectre is dead and the dead are spectral. He elaborates on the "reality effect" in photography[2]:

> I have an even greater sense of the 'real' when what is photographed is a face or a gaze, although in some ways a mountain can be at least as 'real.' The 'reality effect' stems here from the irreducible alterity of another origin of the world. (Derrida and Stiegler 123)

The other opens up another origin of the world.

As Saghafi also argues this sense of alterity in photography is also connected to death. Derrida argues,

> [L]et's say that our relation to another origin of the world or to another gaze, to the gaze of the other, implies a kind of spectrality. Respect for the alterity of the other dictates respect for the ghost [*le revenant*], and, therefore, for the non-living. This is where I try to begin in the book on 'Marx's specters,' when I ask myself how to 'learn how to live' and what 'learning how to live' might mean. (Derrida and Stiegler 123)

Ogier, the whole experience of *Ghost Dance*, its production, its afterlife, connects directly to *Specters of Marx*. In some ways, *Ghost Dance* both precedes and comes after *Specters of Marx*. It follows *Specters* because it is only after *Specters* can we begin to speak to the ghosts around us and try to distinguish, put simply, the good ones from the bad ones. Later, Derrida further drives home the point that spectrality compels us to respect the other origin of the world even if it's destructive, and to see the ghost as something experientially real. This is why he connects the word "specter" with both respect and scepter (as in the king's scepter).

Derrida then asks,

> Respect would be due the law of the other, who appears without appearing and watches or concerns me as a specter, but why would this unconditional authority, which commands duty without duty, without debt, even beyond the categorical imperative, still be figured by the spectral phallus of the king, by the paternal scepter, by an attribute which we would have to obey just as we would the finger and the eye? (Derrida and Stiegler 124)

Indeed, is there a chance that spectrality gives in to the authority of everything that is patriarchal? *Is spectrality a form of male authority?* Of course, spectrality often is of the male gender. In *Archive Fever*, Yerulshami introduces himself into the Freuds by talking about Sigmund's grandfather, adopting his position. By doing that, Yerulshami can have a greater authority over Freud. What is the risk with adorning any and all spectres with male authority? Is this a constant problem of spectrality? It seems to me that if we were discussing the origin of a world, this would be a creative force, equally feminine as well as masculine.

Stiegler then asks about *Specters of Marx* directly. This reality aspect of spectrality is perhaps what compels Stiegler to wonder if spectrality can be linked to a kind of Marxist materialism. Marx, like most of philosophy and science, is in the business of chasing ghosts in order to kill them. Rational discourse tries to make them disappear:

> All of this proceeds from a point where Marx reminds us that the ultimate foundation remains *living* experience, *living* production, which must efface every trace of spectrality. In the final analysis, one must refer to a zone where spectrality is nothing. (Derrida and Stiegler 126–127)

But this being in the now, the living, is also always already technics for Derrida. Specifically referring to television's "real-time" effects, Derrida writes, "[T]he condition of possibility of the living, absolutely real present is already memory, anticipation, in other words, a play of traces. The real-time effect is itself a particular effect of 'différance'" (Derrida and Stiegler 129).

Moments of so-called presence proliferate in *Ghost Dance*. George plays the drum while listening to the radio, as if the weather forecast provided him with the lyrics to a song he had played many times before. Derrida's first cameo also contains moments of sheer spontaneity that seem to give it a reality effect. Sitting in his office, he gives a response to Ogier's question about believing in ghosts:

> The cinema is the art of ghosts, a battle of phantoms. That's what I think the cinema's about, when it's not boring. It's the art of allowing ghosts to come back. That's what we're doing now. Therefore, if I'm a ghost, but believe I'm speaking with my own voice it's precisely because I believe it's my own voice that I allow it to be taken over by another's voice. Not just any other voice, but that of my own ghosts. So ghosts do exist. And it's the ghosts who will answer you. Perhaps they already have. All this, it seems to me, has to do with an exchange between the art of the cinema, in its most original, unedited form and an aspect of psychoanalysis. Cinema plus psychoanalysis equals the Science of Ghosts. You know that Freud ... Freud had to deal all his life with ghosts.

At this point in the monologue, the telephone rings and Derrida without hesitation answers. "Now the telephone is the ghost," he says before providing the voice of the phone with information on the time and location of one of his lectures. He picks up the conversation from there, "Well, that was the phantom voice of someone I don't know. He could have told me any old story. Someone who's arrived from the USA and says he knows a friend of mine. Well, what Kafka says about correspondence, about letters, about epistolary communication also applies to telephonic communication." The postal effect which guarantees indeterminacy of the source rules: the disconnected voice comes from an unknowable space and time in the very moment that it presents itself.

"Mourning and haunting are unleashed at this moment," states Derrida, as if referring to the recording of the interview. "They are unleashed before death itself, out of the mere possibility of death, that is to say, of the trace, which comes into being as immediate sur-vival—and as 'televised'" (Derrida and Stiegler 132). This connects questions of what is beyond the living present, what is spectral, what is inherited to trace and television. In the era of global teletechnology, the powers of mourning and haunting are greater than before. Technology actually denies the safe, comfortable sense of the living moment. On teletechnology, Derrida writes in *Specters*,

> [A]t stake, indissociably, is the differantial deployment of *tekhne*, of techno-science or tele-technology. It obliges us more than ever to think the virtualization of space and time, the possibility of virtual events whose movement and speed prohibit us more than ever (more and otherwise than ever, for this is not absolutely and thoroughly new) from opposing presence to its representation, "real time" to "deferred time," effectivity to its simulacrum, the living to the non-living, in short, the living to the living-dead of its ghosts. (212)

The discussion ends with death and technics: "The law and mourning have the same birthplace, that is to say, death" (Derrida and Stiegler 132). The primary follows the secondary. Technology before nature. Death before life. Mourning and otherness derives from this teletechnological stew.

Having explored spectrality in *Ghost Dance*, *Specters of Marx* and *Echographies of Television*, Derrida therefore knew this Law would be at work in his final collaborations, *D'ailleurs, Derrida* and *Derrida*. Derrida sought film above all to explore and let proliferate spectres. Derrida articulates the ghostly business of cinema in his *Cahiers du cinéma* interview in which mourning, absence and presence of historical and revolutionary figures, and the sheer power of the returning person or thing lost come into play:

> If I had to write on cinema, what would interest me the most would be its mode and system of belief ... In cinema, we believe without believing, but belief without belief remains a belief ... Certain filmmakers attempt to play with these different temporalities of spectres, like Ken McMullen ... There is there elementary spectrality, which is bound to the technical definition of cinema; and within the fictional world, McMullen features characters that are haunted by the history of revolutions, by these ghosts who resurface from history and texts (the communards, Marx, etc.). Cinema thus makes it possible to cultivate what we could call spectral grafts, it inscribes traces of ghosts on a conventional frame, the projected film, which is in itself a ghost ... Spectral memory, cinema is a magnetic mourning, a work of mourning magnified. ("Le cinéma et ses fantômes" 78)[3]

Importantly, voice creates spectrality through its temporality. But how can we think of cinema as a blinding experience? In many ways, this question will occupy the rest of this book. In *Apparitions*, Saghafi explores the connections between photography and *Specters of Marx* and *Echographies of Television*. He writes,

> [T]his ghost is not some wraith that we see coming and going but rather some *one* by whom we feel observed and surveyed, like the law. We are "before the law" when the other looks only at us and there can be no reciprocity or symmetry. Being looked at and watched by law places an infinite demand on me by addressing me solely with an address that is impossible to determine as a request or an order. This regard, Derrida stresses, does not belong merely to the realm of what we too simply call the "living." (55–56)

The other is ghostly for Saghafi because we inherit it, it comes before us, and we can only speak with it through dissymmetry. But photograph and cinema would seem to gather the ghostly qualities of the other more effectively because delay is part of its unique structure of communication. The question of the other's ghostliness comes into full effect with the powers of photography. Derrida writes,

> Louis Marin knew that this authority begins before death, and that death begins its work before death. Death's watch [*veille*], the time of this book, had begun long ago for Louis Marin, well before the eve [*veille*] of his death. (*Work* 164)

Derrida describes the lack of reciprocity in mourning:

> We are speaking of images. What is only in us seems to be reducible to images, which might be memories or monuments, but which are reducible in any case to a memory that consists of visible scenes that are no longer anything but images, since the other of whom they are the images appears only as the one who has disappeared or passed away, as the one who, having passed away, leaves "in us" only images. (*Work* 159)

Following this explanation of the image's connection to mourning, Derrida argues that this image looks at us, concerns us as we internalize it (*Work* 169). The law of inspection produces a gaze that looks at us from within ourselves.

Saghafi finds in Derrida's piece on Louis Marin "By Force of Mourning" many insights that connect photography and spectrality to the powers of responsibility to the other and mourning. He summarizes the situation perfectly:

> This movement of interiorization, Derrida remarks, thus keeps "within us in the form of images" the "life, thought, body, voice, look or soul of the other." Mourning, the desire to remember and retain in memory, then, would be an attempt "which would interiorize within us the image, idol, or ideal of the other." Yet the other "resists the closure of our interiorizing memory," allowing itself only to be interiorized, if at all, as that which cannot be fully interiorized. For interiorization is not possible, must not be possible and completed, if the other is to remain other. (74–75)

Saghafi also relates this to modern visual media: "The structure of the digital, televisual image is spectrally constituted via technological delay. The remote dispatching of 'bodies' that are nonetheless—'artifactual' bodies—is made possible by spectral virtualization" (77). The larger sociocultural implications of mourning and visual culture are rarely discussed in post-structuralism. Derrida, however, is very much interested in exploring these issues in relation to his own collaborations in film. As Saghafi sees it, "Only death—or rather mourning—'can open up this space of absolute *dynamis*' necessary for understanding the powers of the image" (71). It is a mourning activity to consciously adapt Derrida to the moving image. Like he mourned his peers, the filmmakers develop a system of the work of mourning.

Whenever an image of someone is recalled, mourning takes place: "This 'image' is not merely a memory that one has of the friend; it is not how he or she is going to be remembered—he is here, now" (Saghafi 84–85). Mourning begins with the image of the other in me. Saghafi explains the name in Derrida depends on repetition. "The singularity does not forbid the generality from having 'the force of law, but only arrows it, marks, and signs it. Singular plural'" (Saghafi 86). *Punctum* can be a common experience, but it addresses seemingly just me and carries the singularity of the other: "The image of the other—the image that the other inscribed in me—haunts me, is in me, looks at me" (Saghafi 87). Because the *punctum* functions as a personal communication, the presence *seems* greater. Photographic images oscillate between suspense and dependence, according to Saghafi (89).

Instead of talking about the real thing, Saghafi suggests we speak of a spectral structure: "Bearing the signs of death, every photograph speaks of a past anterior" (90). He adds, "It seems everything hinges upon how this 'having-been' is understood" (92). Later, he describes the necessary aporia of photography as a tension between culture and what defies all programmability:

> [A]ll photographs bear the sign of a constant negotiation or rhythmic relation between what is irredeemably other, outside, and the process of technological reproduction, which seeks to interiorize it. Every photograph is thus a constant attempt at capturing the other by luring it into the picture, a relentless pointing to what is singularly other within a graphics of light and shade. (95–96)

"In every photograph there are specters," (93) he claims. The *punctum* and *studium* have a supplementary relationship: while the *punctum* seems to defy planning it can be repeated, so iterable (95). Furthermore, Saghafi explains how the photograph of the other functions similarly to the signature or name:

> Every photograph attests to the return of the dead or departed, the spectral return of the other, like the proper name, which despite having already been distanced from its bearer, always comes back to it. In every photograph I am addressed by the other that comes back, keeps coming back, like a ghost. (93)

The *punctum* is haunted by the possibility of repetition, which makes it into a *studium*. Whereas, the *studium* is haunted by the possibility of the singularity of the other: "This relationship of haunting, where each photograph photographs the other, not only pertains to the *studium* and the *punctum* but applies to every conceptual opposition," (97) claims Saghafi. *Ghost Dance*'s stills are essentially photographs from the film, from scenes, that may or may not have been perceived as *punctums* but that come to stand for something more and in a more common sense: the interchange between *punctum* and *studium*, stillness and motion, occurs equally in cinema as it does in photography proper.

Derrida disrupts standard communication models that maintain viewers are passively viewing images regardless of the nature of the content or that we have mastery over the images we see. He explains,

> One has a tendency to treat what we've been talking about here under the names of image, teletechnology, television screen, archive, as if all these things were on display: a

> collection of objects, things we see, spectacles in front of us, devices we might use, much as we might use a 'teleprompter' we had ourselves prewritten or prescribed. But wherever there are these specters, we are being watched, we sense or think we are being watched. This dissymmetry complicates everything. The law, the injunction, the order, the performative wins out over the theoretical, the constative, knowledge, calculation, and the programmable. (Derrida and Stiegler 122)

This dimension of law adds to communication models not a simplistic propagandistic dimension, but an ethical one. Derrida views all media this way, both "amateur" and "mainstream." The haunting power is an additional force that suggests to simply *believe* in an image has serious ethical consequences.

The recent documentary work of Errol Morris presents an interesting case of spectral cinema. The filmmaker uses a device called the Interrotron, a camera outfitted with a teleprompter with Morris' face projected on it, to interview his subjects. It allows a kind of presence based on eye contact. Morris sits in another room with a camera on him while his face is projected on the screen in front of the camera recording the subject. The eye contact of the participants can only go through the spectralizing experience of projection. The subject is asked to look "at him." "What if I could become one with the camera? What if the camera and myself could become one and the same?" Morris asked himself (Morris). The teleprompter historically contained text that a newsreader would read. "What interests me is that nobody thought of using them for anything other than to display text ... I worried at first. Would it frighten people?" Morris continues (Morris). Essentially, the Interrotron makes it so that we are watching someone watching a film.

Morris has created the ultimate spectral cinema where visibility and invisibility, sight and blindness, presence and absence intersect. Morris' filmmaking is composed of layers of spectres. In Morris' cinematic universe, one is only ever before the law. In *The Fog of War* (2003) and *Standard Operating Procedure* (2008), one doesn't simply have access to the law. Morris makes himself a ghostly presence on set. Morris becomes one with technics, he assumes his fully spectral identity by embodying all others, all viewers, providing layers of otherness between his subject and himself. Always already asymmetrical is the *modus operandi* of his oeuvre. The power of his films doesn't come from the face-to-face, but from spectrality.

In *Fast, Cheap & Out of Control* (1997), eccentric men with obsessional interests in animals, plants, robots relate to us their passions. One of them says, at one point,

> In the ultimate form, all of this stuff is looking at other. The exploring and finding of animals that have absolutely nothing to do with any control that we as a person would have, that feeling that you are in the presence of life that exists irrelevant of yourself,

that's the other. And the other isn't something to be feared. You know, people are afraid of new, different, strange, but to me it isn't anything to be feared. It's something to be wondered at, and looked at, and explored. Perhaps communicated with. Not to sit down and have a conversation, but to take pictures of it and see if you can get the moment where the animal is actually looking at you, and you feel there is a moment of contact. "I know you are. you know I am." It's not something that happens every day. You have to go out and look for it.

Morris has continued to make films in this way. In *Fog of War* and *Standard Operating Procedure* his subjects test our empathy as they reconstruct history through their lenses. The question of belief is always there. Are they believable? Can we believe them?

Derrida defines the teleprompter as a spectral right of inspection in his interview with Laure Adler, explaining, "The word prompter, for it's a word that sends me back to Shakespeare and the theatrical scene, as you know. But now, the prompter, the teleprompter, either way we say it, the teleprompter is part of the current television scene, right. Well, it's subtle."[4] When Adler reminds her guest that there are no teleprompters being used in this interview, he retorts,

> Well apparently, there is no prompter. But there are always because of the sense of urgency of the cameras, all this equipment that they try to make us forget, there are prompter effects. That is to say because I'm here, in the urgency, in a way I'm reading without reading a discourse, the texts which are already in my head pre-established. I have little freedom to invent. And now you in front of me, you are some sort of tele-prompter in your own way. That is to say that I'm trying to speak to you in response not only to your questions, but also within your expectation, like a certain way you seem to dictate a little of the things I'm saying.[5]

Adler interrupts to tell him that he doesn't know the questions she will ask. Derrida counters,

> Even if I try to cheat with the orders given to me by your teleprompter, even if I try to get around the authority of your question, your demand, I am nevertheless forced to keep it in mind. In a way, I am letting myself be dictated already within an extremely particular situation, extremely artificial. What I've been telling you while already speaking too long.[6]

Notes

1. Compared to other philosophers, Derrida left a vast archive of his recorded voice. Many of these recordings are from lectures he gave in the university setting, available at his archives at University of California-Irvine and IMEC.

2. He is likely referring to Barthes, both his essay "The Reality Effect" and his work on photography, primarily in *Camera Lucida*.

3. "Si j'écrivais sur le cinéma, ce qui m'intéresserait surtout serait son mode et son régime de *croyance* ... Au cinéma, on croit sans croire, mais ce croire sans croire reste un croire ...[C]ertains cinéastes essaient de jouer avec ces différentes temporalités des spectres, comme Ken McMullen ... Il y a la spectralité élémentaire, qui est liée à la définition technique du cinéma; et à l'intérieur de la fiction, McMullen met en scène des personnages hantés par l'histoire des révolutions, par ces fantômes qui resurgissent de l'histoire et des textes (les communards, Marx, etc.). Le cinéma permet ainsi de cultiver ce qu'on pourrait appeler des 'greffes' de spectralité, il inscrit des traces de fantômes sur une trame générale, la pellicule projetée, qui est elle-même un fantôme ... Mémoire spectrale, le cinéma est un deuil magnifique, un travail du deuil magnifié."

4. "Moi, le mot prompteur, pour moi c'est un mot qui me renvoie à Shakespeare, au souffleur, à cette scène théâtrale que vous savez. Mais maintenant, le prompteur, le téléprompteur, soit qu'on dit, le téléprompteur fait partie de la scène télévisuelle courante, n'est-ce pas. Alors, c'est subtil."

5. "Donc apparemment il n'y a pas de prompteur. Mais il y a toujours à cause de l'urgence, des caméras, toute cette machinerie qu'on essaye de faire oublier, il y a des effets de prompteur. C'est-à-dire que parce que je suis là, dans l'urgence, d'une part je lis sans lire des discours, des textes qui sont déjà dans ma tête préétablis. J'ai peu de liberté d'invention. Et puis vous en face de moi, vous êtes une sorte de téléprompteur à votre manière. C'est-à-dire que j'essaye de vous parler en répondant non seulement à vos questions, mais à votre attente, comme d'une certaine manière vous, vous me dictez un peu ce que je dis."

6. "Mais même si je triche avec les ordres que me donne votre téléprompteur, même si j'essaie de contourner l'autorité de votre question, votre demande, je suis malgré tout tenu d'en tenir compte. D'une certaine manière, je me laisse dicter déjà dans une situation extrêmement particulière, extrêmement artificielle. Ce que je suis en train de vous dire en parlant déjà trop longtemps."

Bibliography

Barthes, Roland. "The Reality Effect." *The Rustle of Language*. Trans. Richard Howard. New York: Hill and Wang, 1986. 141–148.

Brunette, Peter, and David Wills, eds. *Deconstruction and the Visual Arts: Art, Media, Architecture*. Cambridge and New York: Cambridge University Press, 1994.

Cowie, Elizabeth. *Recording Reality, Desiring the Real*. Minneapolis: University of Minnesota Press, 2011.

Derrida, Jacques. *Dissemination*. Trans. Barbara Johnson. Chicago, IL: University of Chicago Press, 1981.

———. "Le fantôme de l'autre" *Séances* notes. 1984–1985. Jacques Derrida Archives 1949–2004. L'Institut Mémoires de l'édition contemporaine, Basse-Normandie, France.

———. Interview with Laure Adler. *Le cercle de minuit*. France 2. Paris. 23 April 1996.

———. *The Work of Mourning*. Ed. Pascale-Anne Brault and Michael Naas. Chicago, IL: University of Chicago Press, 2001.

———. *Specters of Marx: The State of the Debt, the Work of Mourning, and the New International*. Trans. Peggy Kamuf. New York and London: Routledge, 2006.

Derrida, Jacques, and Bernard Stiegler. *Echographies of Television*. Trans. Jennifer Bajorek. Cambridge: Polity Press, 2002.

Doane, Mary Ann. "The Voice in the Cinema: The Articulation of Body and Space." *Film Theory and Criticism: Introductory Readings*. 5th ed. Ed. Leo Braudy and Marshall Cohen. New York and Oxford: Oxford University Press, 1999. 363–375.

Kittler, Friedrich. *Gramophone, Film, Typewriter*. Trans. Geoffrey Winthrop-Young and Michael Wutz. Stanford, CA: Stanford University Press, 1999.

Leahy, James. "Taking Objective Shape on the Streets: An interview with Ken McMullen." *Monthly Film Bulletin* (1 January 1986): 138–140.

"Le Bon plaisir de Jacques Derrida." *Le Bon plaisir*. Prod. Didier Cahen. France Culture. Paris. 22 March 1986.

McMullen, Ken, dir. *Ghost Dance*. 1983. DVD. Mediabox, 2006a.

———. *Zina*. 1985. DVD. Mediabox, 2006b.

Morris, Errol. "Interrotron." *FLM Magazine* (Winter 2004). http://www.errolmorris.com/content/eyecontact/interrotron.html.

Morris, Errol, dir. *Fast, Cheap & Out of Control*. 1997. DVD. Columbia TriStar Home Entertainment, 2002.

———. *The Fog of War: Eleven Lessons from the Life of Robert S. McNamara*. 2003. DVD. Columbia TriStar Home Entertainment, 2004.

———. *Standard Operating Procedure*. 2008. DVD. Sony, 2008.

Peters, John Durham. *Speaking into the Air: A History of the Idea of Communication*. Chicago and London: University of Chicago Press, 1999.

Saghafi, Kas. *Apparitions—Of Derrida's Other*. New York: Fordham University Press, 2010.

Secret, Timothy. *The Politics and Pedagogy of Mourning: On Responsibility in Eulogy*. London: Bloomsbury, 2015.

CHAPTER FOUR

3rd *Séance*: Before the Law of Spectrality: Derrida on the Prague Imprisonment

There are many ways to delimit the subject of the image in Derrida—including as a form of blindness, a work of mourning, and the right of inspection. A revealing task would be to carefully ponder some of Derrida's images of himself and his own theories of the visual. Such a study would show how Derrida's embrace of the visual resulted in a completely unique public image. A kind of blind or ghostly philosophical persona rubs up against the linearity and solidity of the philosophical project itself. There are several photographic portraits of Jacques Derrida where blindness seems to take centre stage. This chapter charts Derrida's performances in front of the camera and argues that several different film retellings of his 1982 imprisonment in Prague articulate the connections between blindness, spectrality, and Law. The Prague imprisonment incident seemed to go hand-in-hand with revoking his self-imposed ban on his public image, beginning with his first television interview on Antenne 2. He briefly describes the fact that guards made references to Kafka during his imprisonment in the essay "Before the Law" (1982) and, in *Ghost Dance* (dir. McMullen, 1983), he reveals that he was researching on Kafka at the very moment of his arrest.

Before examining each version of the incarceration in turn, I will attempt to contextualize several notable "blind" (auto) portraits of Derrida. Such critical analysis is meant to lay some foundation of the philosopher's accounts of the experience of being photographed. In a 2002 *LA Weekly* interview, Derrida explains,

> I succeeded in publishing for almost twenty years without a single image of myself appearing in connection with my books, and there were two reasons for that. First, I had what you might describe as ideological objections to the conventional author photograph—a head shot, or a picture of the writer at his desk—because it struck me as a concession to selling and to media. (Dick and Ziering Kofman, *Derrida* 124)

Derrida continues,

> The second reason was that I've always had a difficult relationship with my own body and image. It's hard for me to look at myself in photographs, so for twenty years I gave myself permission to erase my image on political grounds. Over the last decade, that became increasingly difficult because I was constantly appearing in public spaces at conferences attended by journalists, many of whom took pictures. It finally became impossible to control, and as I felt it was time to overcome this resistance I finally let it go. (Dick and Ziering Kofman, *Derrida* 124)

His reluctance to have his photograph publicly disseminated for years came to an end seemingly overnight. He went from a degree zero of images of the self to a multiplicity of images and did so quite rapidly and consciously following the Prague affair. He also began writing on the visual and photography more routinely at this point. A rare phenomenon in the life of a major philosopher at the time, this practise invited the scorn of other academics (see Peeters 442–443; Shumway; Lamont).

In "The Star System in Literary Studies," David R. Shumway argues a Hollywood-like star system was created in academic literary studies in the 1960s and was fully operational by the 1990s. According to him, it poses a threat to collective scholarship and often produces undeserved authority (98). The introduction of a so-called star system in the academy also means that performative practises become central to the construction of a body of work (96). Derrida's public performances would have begun in the academy, especially at conferences. Performances become key to the academic self, and Derrida is the best example of this, argues Shumway:

> Derrida is *the* jet-set academic, a professor who seems to spend more time in the air between gigs than on the ground at any particular job … Each performance—to the extent that it is successful—extends Derrida's personality further into the terrain of intellectual life. (95–96)

Unique personality becomes the new barometer for success for "stars" like Fish, Derrida, and Spivak.

Cultural myths of individual academic genius have been in circulation for years. In "The Brain of Einstein," Barthes argues that our fascination with Einstein is due to a mythic operation wherein we assign magical properties to Einstein's brain. This fetishization of his brain is actually due to our current space-bias and our embrace of speed in intellectual life. Photographs, cartoons, and other popular media often show Einstein within contexts of the university or the classroom or laboratory, standing beside a blackboard full of complex formulas. The myth of Einstein is that knowledge is produced quickly and yet it is complete (Barthes, *Mythologies* 69). Foucault, too, saw through the ideological function often given to the individual author of note, saying, "[I]f we are accustomed to presenting the author as a genius, as a perpetual surging of invention, it is because, in reality, we make him function in exactly the opposite fashion" ("What is an Author?" 119). The creation of a single author or genius is a way for a culture to use a discourse about the author in order to do certain things, to ensure certain censorships, one is tempted to say—"The author is therefore the ideological figure by which one marks the manner in which we fear the proliferation of meaning" (Foucault, "What is an Author?" 119).

Sociologist Michèle Lamont argues to understand the legitimation of deconstruction "it is necessary to identify channels of diffusion." She writes, "[C]ultural products are not diffused in unified markets but rather among actors whose definition of good work segments cultural markets" (608). This is an apt approach to studying a major philosopher who participated in multiple media productions and published widely in US and France as it allows us to understand the specific sociocultural contexts of each of these cultural artefacts. As a whole, the films of Jacques Derrida tell us many things about an important part of the philosopher's life. They do everything from offer opportunities to explain, and bear witness to, philosophy to a wide public (as in his television interviews), to experiment with the cinematic medium (as in the art house film *Ghost Dance*), and to negotiate the dynamics of the documentarian-subject, or guest-host, binary (like in 2002s biographical *Derrida*). In each of these works, a different audience is addressed for a different market.

Previous studies of intellectuals in the popular media, like Marcie Frank's *How to be an Intellectual in the Age of TV: The Lessons of Gore Vidal* and Tamara Chaplin's *Turning on the Mind: French Philosophers on Television*, have performed careful close analyses of media content to tell national histories of intellectual or philosophical debates. Frank uses theories of the intellectual from Foucault ("Two Lectures"), Said, Posner, and others to situate Gore Vidal as a highly media-literate public intellectual who understood the requirements of the talk show but wasn't afraid to treat it as a venue for intellectual debate and clarity (42). The long history of publicly funded philosophy programs on French television is brilliantly illuminated in the Chaplin study, as she recounts the numerous debates, performances, and stylistic devices of *Lectures pour tous* (1953–1968), *L'enseignement de la philosophie*,

Apostrophes (1975–1990), and other programs. France's most prominent intellectuals, such as Sartre, Camus, Bachelard, Jeanson, Aron, and Foucault, all appeared on *Lectures pour tous*, which aired from 1953 to 1968, debating and disseminating philosophy.

Derrida didn't appear in the media until relatively late in his career. Many of the media texts that he would participate in were in fact established genres, such as avant-garde film, the TV book talk show, and documentary film. In order to demonstrate why media producers were interested in Derrida and why Derrida saw many of them as opportunities to integrate deconstruction and cinema, my study performs textual analysis of films and television shows and draws on filmmakers' interpretations, theoretical concepts from deconstruction theory, and film criticism to paint a cultural and philosophical picture of a popular intellectual collaborating with filmmakers and producers to communicate philosophical ideas.

Lamont's 1987 article "How to Become a Dominant French Philosopher: The Case of Jacques Derrida" incorporates biographical information, contemporaneous histories of philosophy in France, literature on the sociology of French intellectuals, and findings from interviews to mount her critique of Derrida and the legitimation of deconstruction in both France and US. While her study never adequately delves into the significance and complexity of deconstruction, Lamont offers an interesting model for similar case studies of intellectuals in the media. The article sees cultural capital as a determining force and the reason why Derrida became a prominent philosopher. Derrida's success was partly due to the rise of other French philosophers after 1968, each of whom had their own set of grand theories to offer the upper-middle class intelligentsia in France (592), even though by Lamont's own admission, Derrida did not actively seek wide media coverage like some of his peers (598). Deconstruction was successfully packaged as an exotic cultural good and disseminated through journals, schools, cultural media, and associations (600). Lamont critiques the high value placed on deconstruction theory by both Derrida and his peers (i.e. journalists, scholars, writers, artists). I will use a similar case study approach to study the kind of media (film, television, print, others) and media practises (production and distribution) that aided Derrida in his rise to prominence. But if we supplemented Lamont's approach with Chaplin's, we begin to see how an approach that delves deeper into the issues and circumstances that surround each cultural artefact helps tell the history of modern philosophy and in particular the development of deconstruction.

As Tamara Chaplin shows, television played an important role in the dissemination of philosophy in French society in the second half of the 20th century. By the mid-1970s shows like *Apostrophes* played a significant role in boosting sales of philosophy books (133). Some were not happy with the way these shows represented philosophical discussion and how they seemed to popularize a certain entertaining brand of philosophy: "Ever since Apostrophes first appeared, intellectuals have critiqued the structure of television debate as hostile to considered intellectual and philosophical exchange. This format, they argue, lacks intellectual flexibility, censoring thoughtful discussion and accelerating dialogue" (137). Derrida would turn his attention to the telegenic philosophy more and more from the early 1990s onward. His exchanges with Laure Adler and Bernard Stiegler were replete with self-reflexive observations of the filming process itself and how he often felt intellectuals were undone by the format.

Still many intellectuals appeared on these programs to get their messages out. Foucault appeared on *Apostrophes* on 17 December 1976 and famously interrupted the discussion of his books to talk about the KGB's prosecution of a doctor for sexual misconduct in 1974—also known as the "Stern affair." Chaplin observes,

> Demonstrating through his actions the very dynamic he sought to illustrate with his words, Foucault subverted the power of the media and deployed it to his own ends. Ignoring the unspoken rules governing the host/guest interaction, Foucault overrode convention, diverting the focus and directing both guests and the television audience towards the issues (both political and philosophical), that he deemed important. (142)

Later, Chaplin adds, "His actions on the broadcast implied not a rejection of the media but rather an explicit embrace of its demands. Indeed, Foucault appropriated both the medium (television) and the message (the Gulag), choosing a major media event in order to drive his ideas home" (143). There is a sense that Foucault added a counter-discourse to the program yet his relevant message fit nicely within the dominant style of television at the time.

Since the mid-1970s there has been generally more media attention paid to the "New Philosophers." At the same time the documentary program *Les idées et les hommes* started producing portraits of great philosophers, including Plato, Spinoza, and Kierkegaard. The question of the image or biography of the philosopher was analyzed by Jean-François Lyotard in a program called *Tribune libre* on 27 March 1978. For Lyotard, the image or representation of the philosopher was problematic. He questioned why philosophy would need an image of an individual at all, and who decides who gets to appear as an authoritative philosopher. He also claims, "For a long time in the West, philosophers have been exposed to the temptation of the role of the intellectual, they have been tempted to turn themselves into the representatives of an authority" (Chaplin 172). Yet he chose to argue this point by using his image in a decidedly experimental way, using superimpositions, playing with the image of his name over his three heads, creating sound and image disparities, and, by turning his back to the camera as he says, "He doesn't just write books, he's professor of philosophy at the University of Vincennes; so he does philosophy. No one has ever been quite sure what that consists of" (171). Chaplin concludes,

> [T]he contents of the program call into question the effects of the form while simultaneously reinforcing these effects. For, even as Lyotard uses the broadcast to question the role of the intellectual, his very presence on the screen accentuates his special status. (173)

While Chaplin calls Lyotard's segment a "tour de force," it hardly constitutes a continued engagement with the medium.

In a sense, Derrida haunts this era precisely by not appearing on any of these programs in the 1970s and early 1980s. Is his absence from philosophical talk shows truly a self-imposed restriction or does deconstruction not meet the ends of the debate format that would become the norm? Is it simply too difficult to place deconstruction within a political debate where two people square off? Could deconstruction excel in either traditional political terms or even ethical terms of the New Philosophers? And finally: what to make of his initial "absence" and his later multiple appearances and cinematic collaborations?

Deleuze also tapped into the power of the spectral forces of modern cinematography and telecommunications when he agreed to a long *Abécédaire* with the proviso that it be aired on television after his death:

> L'enregistrement du direct est ici métamorphosé en possibilité d'éternité mais, alors que, dans la plupart des situations télévisuelles, cette condition constitue au mieux une sorte d'impensé, au pire un gâchis, ici, elle est parfaitement assumée et devient une arme pour penser. Deleuze se fait future archive audiovisuelle, et en jouit comme d'un privilège tout à fait exorbitant. (Jousse 20)[1]

Deleuze's approach to the study of cinema in his *Cinema 1 & 2* books consisted of articulating types of image, based on concepts, such as time-, movement-, crystal-images. Deleuze of course never imagines himself as a filmmaker or subject and even takes his own biographical details out of the analysis of individual films, much like in traditional philosophical discourse. But whereas Derrida embraced autobiography in his work, Deleuze limited the degree of biographical content in his work as a philosopher. Deleuze rarely made his personal life public; he did even less media appearances than most of his peers, such as Foucault, Bourdieu, and Derrida.

While highly critical of the influx of marketing thinking in society in general, Deleuze and Guattari point out the importance of the conceptual persona within philosophical discourse. One of philosophy's main pursuits is the conceptual persona, which allows the philosophical discourse to relate to people. The development of a new concept on a plane of immanence needs this persona, which is both fictional and non-fictional, according to Deleuze and Guattari. The conceptual personae contain important elements for a philosophy to take formation, such as geographical and identity issues. They write,

> Conceptual personae are the philosopher's 'heteronyms,' and the philosopher's name is the simple pseudonym of his personae ... The destiny of the philosopher is to become his conceptual persona or personae, at the same time that these personae themselves become something other than what they are historically, mythologically, or commonly ... (64)

Do Deleuze and Guattari not make explicit room for the work of mourning within their conception of the conceptual persona when they write about the importance of not following in the "Friend's" footsteps:

> "[T]he Friend," but a friend who has a relationship with his friend only through the thing loved, which brings rivalry ... Not two friends who communicate and recall the past together but, on the contrary, who suffer an amnesia or aphasia capable of splitting thought, of dividing it in itself. Personae proliferate and branch off, jostle one another and replace each other? (70–71)

What if a philosopher's conceptual persona avoided the supposed concreteness and determinacy of Plato's Socrates or Nietzsche's Antichrist? What if the job of the philosopher wasn't to offer a persona but alterity? Derrida's "Ghost" persona questions the very homogeneity of such a construct. What is even more thrilling is that he did this in the movies.

By pointing out the ideologies inherent in television, Derrida adopts the role of reflexive media intellectual in his television appearances and experiments with the medium in a similar way to his work in *Ghost Dance*. One resulted in the collaborative project *Echographies of Television*. Originally intended as a television broadcast, the 1993-filmed interview between Derrida and Bernard Stiegler was later transcribed and released as a book. Another noteworthy text is the 23 April 1996 aired interview with Laure Adler on her show *Cercle de minuit* on France 2. These two programs touch on Derrida's key thoughts and criticisms on the medium and benefit from his attentiveness to the recording process and his reflexive commentaries on television. In the televised interviews, Derrida considers the nature of time associated with the medium. Àpropos the Adler interview, the *Nouvel observateur* would publish a rave review, stating, "It was pure magic! A completely new freedom of expression, a fresh style of thinking, new paths boldly opened up ... I've never seen anything like it before" (Peeters 480).

There is a certain complexity about the topic of Derrida's participations in the media in particular. He was the philosopher that pointed out hierarchies implicit in communication—speech and writing, sound and visual. In *Dissemination*, he questions the distinction between speech and writing as presented in Plato's *Phaedrus*:

> Plato is following certain rhetors and sophists before him who, as a contrast to the cadaverous rigidity of writing, had held up the living spoken word, which infallibly conforms to the necessities of the situation at hand, to the expectations and demands of the interlocutors present, and which sniffs out the spots where it ought to produce itself, feigning to bend and adapt at the moment it is actually achieving maximum persuasiveness and control. (79)

Similarly, television has been described as a primarily sound medium (Altman), while film's authority derives from the image while sound is relegated to a supplementary status (Doane). Liveness and *vérité* aesthetics each offer viewers a sense of spontaneity and unfolding reality. Derrida analyzed the metaphysics of presence in philosophy for many years before he became what one might call a media philosopher. But his writings on modern media are no less important.

A boom in philosophy in France explains why much cultural media, including television, reached a new plateau in 1990s: "By the late 1990s it seemed that you couldn't turn on a French TV set without laying eyes on a philosopher. And television was not alone in its predilection for the discipline. Philosophy was, literally and visually, everywhere" (Chaplin 226). *D'ailleurs, Derrida* was produced in this cultural context where French culture embraced and gave voice to its philosophers. Derrida, as previously stated, was actually a rare philosophical spectacle, having done relatively little television. This absence eventually did end when Derrida agreed to two major autobiographical documentaries later in life. In addition to working on two feature films with him as the subject, he allowed Safaa Fathy to film many of his lectures at l'École des Hautes Études en Sciences Sociales.[2]

Why capture an intellectual's personality on film? And is that even what the documentaries and portraits of academics and philosophers do? Do they dwell on pseudo-events and affective dimensions of their subjects? Documentaries about public intellectuals, including *Manufacturing Consent* (dir. Mark Achbar and Peter Wintonick, Australia/Finland/Norway/Canada, 1992) and *Žižek!* (dir. Astra Taylor, US/Canada, 2005) routinely follow their subjects on the conference circuit or show them being interviewed in the media, and therefore provide a doubled space for the academic to negotiate his or her unique persona. These films often creatively reveal how each scholar negotiates an academic star image in unique but overlapping ways. But what makes the 2002 biography of Derrida special or different is its delirious reflexivity that marks its constructedness in advance and the way it performs textually the decentring of the subject.

Today, photographs and images of the modern academic ceaselessly proliferate on university faculty websites, in conference catalogues, on YouTube, and on social and professional media sites. There is not just one image, but many. Photography is one way that the modern academic can get noticed. But being photographed can be a deeply objectifying experience. Talking with Derrida on photography, Hubertus von Amelunxen observes the following: "One is photographable, 'photogenic,' and this is perhaps the catastrophe, that one can be photographable, that one can be captured and caught in time" (*Copy* 36). Barthes has produced some of the most resonant insights on this topic. His thoughtful description accounts for many nuances of being photographed:

> In front of the lens, I am at the same time: the one I think I am, the one I want others to think I am, the one the photographer thinks I am, and the one he makes use of to exhibit his art. In other words, a strange action: I do not stop imitating myself, and because of this, each time I am (or let myself be) photographed, I invariably suffer from a sensation of inauthenticity, sometimes of imposture (comparable to certain nightmares). In terms of image-repertoire, the Photograph (the one I intend) represents that very subtle moment when, to tell the truth, I am neither subject nor object but a subject who feels he is becoming an object: I then experience a micro-version of death (of parenthesis): I am truly becoming a specter. (*Camera* 14–15)

This production of the spectre makes photography (its production, its dissemination) into a profoundly complex act. Derrida, it could be said, has a motivated approach to the image. The image must be fully thought out and considered before it is taken. For him, the photograph can be a matter of archiving (work of mourning), like in the case of Jean-François Bonhomme's photographs of Athens, or communication, where its intersubjective nature becomes prominent. The image of the philosopher is even more motivated. Philosophers used to trade portraits of themselves, and they would often sign them. Derrida argues, "Today one thinks of stars, celebrities of the image and the spectacle, signing photographs. It would be rare, and ridiculous, for a 'thinker' to do this now" (*Copy* 22). He is fully aware that portraits of the modern academic turn them into a sign that then does a certain kind of work in culture and the culture of the university.

1979 was a turning point of sorts for Derrida and his public image. He first chose to publicize his image at the same time that he warned against the media philosophy that was infiltrating the culture. Events surrounding the Estates General of Philosophy at the Sorbonne in June brought together many academics to discuss the status of philosophy in France. The events were publicized by the press, and Derrida took this public occasion to represent the philosophical community (Bennington and Derrida 334). Derrida was bothered by popular philosophy in France and criticized the philosophy of the market (of the media), calling it "ignorant" and "unforgivably boring" (*Who's Afraid* 180). The point wasn't to champion the philosophy of the university classroom while denigrating popular philosophy, however:

> It would be a serious mistake on our part to ignore the fact that when we are often shocked or made indignant by certain of these effects, it is because, even in our bodies, we live our relation to philosophy behind very selective protecting filters, in laboratories whose social, political, and philosophical condition deserves to be interrogated just as much as the one that produces, in newspapers and on television, some philosophy or something that, despite everything, retains a resemblance with philosophy. (*Who's Afraid* 181–182)

In his first public images, he was signified as *philosophe engagé*, maintaining this important French discipline, a proponent of high philosophy, and a warrior against philosophical charlatans. In one photo, he can be seen arguing vehemently with Bernard-Henry Lévy.

When he was wrongfully arrested and detained in Prague in 1981 for drug trafficking, he appeared on national television for the first time to explain the experience of his arrest and the reason why he was there: to attend a clandestine seminar in support of Czech intellectuals (Bennington and Derrida 334). There is nothing to suggest that these initial appearances in the public eye were planned or deliberate. The following year, he would star in the McMullen film with Ogier. But up until this time, he had maintained the ban on his public image, even resisting including a portrait on his book covers. Importantly, he had appeared in the public eye as an intellectual, bearing witness to his experiences related to his intellectual community and philosophical life.

Derrida and other scholars that have made photography an essential philosophical subject evoke issues like aura and presence (an especially tricky issue for deconstruction) to account for the phenomenology of the medium (see Benjamin). There are several ways of talking about the image in Derrida, whether as blindness, work of mourning, or the right of inspection. A revealing task would be to carefully ponder some of Derrida's images of himself and his own theories of the visual. Such a study would show how Derrida's embrace of the visual meant a completely unique public image for a philosopher. *The Truth in Painting* book cover photograph, which also appeared in the 1986 *New York Times Magazine* article "The Tyranny of the Yale Critics," offers an instructive case of the "star" philosopher's portrait. Shumway describes it thus:

> While the other photos contextualize their subjects, Derrida dominates this scene, the background being dark and serving to frame the figure. The chiaroscuro lighting dramatically features one side of his face as he leans forward and offers an indistinct expression, one similar to [J. Hillis] Miller's but made more dramatic by the lighting. Even Derrida's clothing is dramatic—a black corduroy jacket rather than the usual

tweed sport coat—and it also serves to set off the star's face … Derrida is presented like a movie star. (91)

Regrettably, Shumway fails to mention how the photograph was used for the publication of *The Truth in Painting* and how it ties in with many of the ideas developed therein. The whole purpose of the book was to advocate for more thoughtful, complex interpretations of visual culture. The failure of Derrida's critics, it seems to me, has to do with the difference between engaging deconstruction and studying its institutional validity.

In *Droit de regards*, the pose [*mise en demeure*] emerges as a unique and purposive characteristic of the photographic medium because it is among many things a way to use the body as an address. In an average pose, the "character" (they are all too real) gives the right of inspection to the photographer or the apparatus or the viewer. On posing for the camera, Derrida notes,

> *Mise en demeure* is an untranslatable expression because it concerns the law. It concerns legitimacy, one's *entitlement* to look, to arrange or hold within one's gaze, to take in a view, or to 'take' a photograph—hence it concerns the title, *droit de regards*. (Derrida and Plissart 2)

Normally, when the viewer views this performance, a right has been afforded. The right of inspection can set into motion countless addresses, narratives, readings—this is the right of inspection—but there are specific addresses too. To paraphrase the Barthes of *Camera Lucida*, there is always an intentional aspect of the photograph; for him, it exists within the dimension of the referent. These rights all mix together, creating what might be called cycles of meaning and responsibility.

If we were to understand Derrida's portrait more fully than his critics allow, we would start to appreciate the extent to which he and his collaborators were able to introduce artistic endeavours into the philosophical discipline. In the photograph described by Shumway, dark columns frame Derrida. He is thus framed twice. But he also leans forward, as if he were stepping out of the frame. The dark, abyssal background conjures a nightmarish quality. His slightly tousled hair implies a gust of wind, and the way the frame cuts the large trees in the background gives the sense of the sublime. There is also the impression that Derrida steps out of the abyss, as we are left to contemplate it. It is Derrida's half-lit face that is presumably closest to us. Out of the abyss—*chiaroscuro*—into the light, his face and his hands are there for us. *To greet us?*

In *Truth in Painting*, the *parergon* and the frame are supports and often blur conventional notions of inside and outside. He writes about the size of the colossal and questions the logic of scale in Kant's explanation of the sublime:

> The sublime quality of the colossal, although it does not derive from art or culture, nevertheless has nothing natural about it. The cise of the colossus is neither culture nor nature, both culture and nature. It is perhaps, between the presentable and the unpresentable, the passage from one to the other as much as the irreducibility of the one to the other. (143)

The colossal is both subjective and objective. "The column is of average, moderate, measurable, measured size. The measure of its erection can be taken. In this sense it would not be colossal, the column," (122) he explains. The columns, the parerga, enlarge the background and the foreground. According to Shumway, the columns frame Derrida perfectly. But actually, Derrida, with his back turned toward the *small* columns, takes on at one and the same time a fragile and larger-than-life aura. He can't be contained yet there is at least an effort to do so. His body language, his slightly bent back (always facing the nightmarish skyline) creates a sense of shelter in front of him. Take shelter in my eyes and in my hands, the photograph seems to say.

Shumway frames him at once, like a movie star's close-up. "Like a movie star": Not an artist or an intellectual, but a celebrity. Shumway easily falls for the trap of allowing the columns to frame the star. In fact what really creates the impression of a celebrity is the jacket. It doesn't resemble the apparel of the average professor, even though it too is corduroy. Perhaps it is the banded collar that screams charlatan. Shumway frames Derrida in precisely the same way different interpreters frame Van Gogh's shoes. Is it Van Gogh's signature, or Heidegger or Shapiro's interpretations that create a frame? Shumway owes us culprits—academic celebrities—the outlaw and the authority figure. This single image allows Shumway to question the legitimacy of the entire discipline of literary studies. The function of the photo in Shumway is equivalent to the Reward poster of the Old West. Furthermore, the thumb poking out of the sleeve where the sex would be introduces another important theme. As if he predicted Shumway's criticisms, Derrida already accounts for nakedness in the Donoso photograph. Talking about the way the photographed individual gives up a certain access to themselves, Derrida says, "[T]his is a gesture that can in certain situations be more exposed, more giving and more intense than 'making love.' In it the gaze is naked, at once naked and not seeing itself. Exposed as overexposed, like nudity" (*Copy* 32–33). Derrida reveals himself, nothing left to hide. He admits his absolute nakedness. In this case, the photographic portrait is associated with nakedness but also with hospitality.

Referring to the book he wrote with Geoffrey Bennington, *Jacques Derrida*, Derrida speaks about his initial idea to publish the book with a scanned image of the inside of his skull instead of the conventional medium-close shot of the head and shoulders. Derrida observes, "The 'great actors'... could not have entertained this hypothesis or this game: to inscribe a dedication on the image of their skull. They could not do this and no doubt would not have wanted or dared to" (*Copy* 38). The inside of the skull fails to reproduce the part of the body that retains one's singular otherness: the face. But the fact that he entertained the idea reveals the artistic and creative thought that he put into his photographic portraits. He was ready to challenge the generic conventions of the author's photograph because he knew full well that even the most natural image is altered by invention, thus corrupting authenticity. But he often opted for photography as discovery of a singular otherness assisted by the photographer's productive imagination, of course. Is Derrida's reflexivity a form of mourning in advance? To what extent is spectrality inscribed in these photographs and in Derrida's writings on the subject? Does he not want to leave an image of himself in philosophy? The skull photograph is his most deathly proposal yet in his writing on the visual arts.

In *Truth in Painting*, Derrida via Benjamin isolates a single aspect of the portrait that still bears a cultural imprint:

> The photographic representation of the face is the remainder, the last resistance of ritual. When the face begins to disappear or ... no longer to occupy the top or the center, the legend becomes necessary ... When the 'exhibition value' fractures the 'cult value', the latter retreats and entrenches itself in the human face. (178–179)

The camera captures the mechanical looking at wherein the person being photographed can't see his or her own gaze. The subject's gaze still haunts us in the "age of technological reproducibility." Photography subjects are momentarily blind to themselves. Benjamin touches on the same point when he writes, "Photography, with its devices of slow motion and enlargement, reveals this posture to him. He first learns of this optical unconscious through photography, just as he learns of the instinctual unconscious through psychoanalysis" (278–279). Derrida says, we give up our narcissism in the activities of photography: "I give as if I were giving myself, as if I were giving even my impossible narcissism" (*Copy* 32).

Benoît Peeters describes a photo shoot Derrida agreed to do with Carlos Freire for an article in *Le Magazine littéraire* in 1991:

> The Brazilian photographer showed him at home, in his office, in his attic; we can see his collection of pipes, his little Citroën; we meet him in a café on the boulevard Raspail, just before his seminar at the École de Hautes Études, in the lecture hall with students, then in a salon of the Hôtel Lutétia. In spite of all his friendliness towards the photographer, Derrida lent himself to the image rather than abandoning himself to it. (442)

This anxiety would re-emerge often, and sometimes become full-on resistance. For Derrida, in addition to the sense of nakedness, the photographic experience also produces blindness (and anxiety one would guess). He brings this aspect of its phenomenology into play in a 2002 photograph taken by Serge Picard that is featured in Peeters' biography. Derrida, in a black suit and unbuttoned white shirt, stands slightly hunched, "like a boxer" (Peeters 442). He is softly lit from the left side. His white hair and shirt pop out. The expression on his face is solemn, and his eyes are shut (or only very slightly opened). In one of the last photographs of Derrida, he stands in near complete darkness, with only a half-lit face. The photograph dramatizes blindness perfectly. One of his last photos registers his concerns about the indeterminacy of his portrait, his public image.

To give a photograph of oneself becomes an act of hospitality. Derrida explains with a certain tenderness:

> To a friend I can offer a photograph of my house, of my study and my work table, or even of my books, a photograph that would thus have a value of hospitality. Photography is still marked by all the possibilities of *Dasein*. (*Copy* 28)

With photography, there is still a certain attachment to the life-giving qualities of the world—something remains. Photography, as a cultural activity of disclosure, can be an invitation given to the other by the other. It is a cultural meeting ground, and in the past, it was the first encounter. If photography can do this, then it does it instantaneously. Photographic images will become an increasingly important part of Derrida's philosophy itself, and the more he collaborates with filmmakers and other artists, the more images proliferate, the more meaning disseminates.

Spectrality is about knowing that one is blind before the other. In a spectral communication model, the audience will always remain out of reach, other. Both the book and Louvre exhibit *Memoirs of the Blind* argue that sight is conditioned on the occasion of blindness, that is, the blink or wink or indeed near- and far-sightedness (Derrida, *Memoirs* 48). In the museum documentary of the exhibit of the same name, Derrida acts out how the artist does a self-portrait he reveals how it is strictly speaking an encounter with the other. The subject, like all the viewers to come, is temporarily blinded. Derrida acts out the movements of the subjects of the drawings, especially those about outreached hands. In the autoportrait, the spectator replaces the artist. He sees his blindness, and this is the point at which the other enters the scene. Derrida looks at the camera while talking about the law of impossible blindness. The drawing becomes a kind of mourning work: the artist is forced to replace himself by the other (Fargier [1990] 1992). To be seen by the other (who is also yourself) means to see the alterity within yourself. It follows then that film for Derrida was thus a way of feeling, sensing, experiencing, and understanding the self as other.

De mon vu, the way I see it, the visible is the end, the final stage. Indeed, the visible is murderous as it forecloses life. Derrida reminds us that the point of view technically relies on a blind spot: "Speaking of perspectivism, it's to say that we always see things, that we always interpret things from a certain point of view, based on an interest by cutting out a schema of vision, which is organized, hierarchized, a schema which is always selective, and that consequently, owes as much to blindness as to vision" (*Penser* 64).[3] Even when looking at myself in the mirror, I cannot see myself seeing:

> We do not see our eyes *simultaneously* as seeing *and* visible. [...] In the experience of the mirror, this indecision flourishes. When we look at ourselves in the mirror we must choose between looking at the colour of our eyes and looking at the flux, the spilling out of the gaze that looks at itself with all the paradoxes of the auto-portrait. (Derrida, *Penser* 63)[4]

One cannot see one's own gaze, and therefore the other sees us. Blindness, the other, sees.

The connection between spectrality and mourning (the self) is also developed in Derrida's critique of Freud in "Legs de Freud" from *The Post Card*, where he shows how the Fort/Da game represents a perpetual absence/presence. The Fort/Da game was spelled out after Freud observed the behaviour of his grandson who tied a wooden spool to a piece of string and began to throw the spool over the bed and bring it back again over and over. For Freud, this game was a way for his grandson to symbolically bring back his mother who was often leaving him alone. Derrida points out that the child's serious game reflects Freud's own personal feelings about his own absent daughter, the mother, who died young. Derrida questions whether the pleasure principle rules the scenario. He writes about the power of the return itself:

> [W]hat binds the game to itself is the *re-* of the return, the additional turn of repetition and re-appearance. He insists upon the fact that the greatest quantity of pleasure is in the second phase, in the *re*-turn which orients the whole, and without which nothing would come. *Revenance*, that is, returning, orders the entire teleology. (*Post* 317)

Then later he adds, "One must make return the repetition of that which returns, and must do so on the basis of its returning" (*Post* 318).

The return of representation, of a repetition compulsion doesn't just produce pleasure from the returning of the presence, but the return of that which is completely other. The returning gathers teleological powers:

> What will return [*reviendra*], in having already come, but not in order to contradict the PP, nor to oppose itself to the PP, but to mine the PP as its proper stranger, to

> hollow it into an abyss from the vantage of an origin more original than it and inde-
> pendent of it, older than it within it, will not be, under the name of the death drive
> or the repetition compulsion, an *other master or a counter-master*, but something other
> than mastery, something completely other. (*Post* 317–318)

Derrida doesn't quite explain the significance of this completely other in *The Post Card*. But if I had to speculate, this other would be spectrality itself. If the thing—*spectre*—weren't other, it would already be present, that is, known, assimilated, and, thus, unworthy of respect. This return of the other is also the reappearing of the other *in you*: "[T]he child identifies himself with the mother since he disappears as she does, and makes her return with himself, by making himself return without making anything but himself, her in himself, return" (*Post* 319). To be even more precise, "He speaks *to himself* telephonically, he calls himself, recalls himself, 'spontaneously' affects himself with his presence-absence in the presence-absence of his mother" (*Post* 319).

If while watching a film, the film's referent is the ghost, making a film suggests something else: we are interiorized by the ghost who sees us, concerns us—the ghost's crypt. The ghost is also haunted by all the possible viewers, spectators. They too are haunted. We occupy the role of spectator-spectre. That's what Derrida wants to say: absence is the thing we have in common. The spectre looks at an us that is spectral. We are addressed as indeterminate, absent. No one is present. No one. In *Ex-Cinema: From a Theory of Experimental Film and Video*, Akira Mizuta Lippit suggests the same when he writes on the spectre as a form of blindness in the autobiography film genre, where he describes life as a series of encounters with the spectral self. Lippit explains,

> The trope of blindness—abundant in Derrida's work to the point of a theme—and the
> figure of the blind emerge most often for Derrida in the form of a paradox: blindness
> is the mechanism or condition through which one sees oneself. I am blind to myself,
> but this blindness is revelatory: it reveals me to myself, and it reveals my blindness as
> a condition and precondition of seeing myself. (92)

Lippit suggests that life is misremembering former impressions of the self, or a lack of memory of the self, hence the self haunts the self, or the self renders the self blind. The self sees you, but you are blind to the self. What seems to be missing from writing on Derrida's film work is how the performances comment on the old ones, fold into each other, how they speak to each other—in short, defer. In the 2002 documentary, the self could be described as unmaking the self. Filmmaking becomes an opportunity to unmake a coherent self, to encounter the unmade self.

The spectre isn't reciprocal or tangible. A form of internalization of the other, mourning internalizes images of the other; that's what mourning does and how it relates to identity (Lippit 93). But this renders us blind to ourselves when we are in the other's gaze. The other is in us, dividing, puncturing our coherent identities. Lippit confirms the existence of ghosts as anterior to knowledge. Lippit's definition of spectrality hinges on (in)visibility: "Visible and invisible are not antitheses of visuality as such … They are positive forms of the image—visible and invisible images—superimposed over one another and generating a secret medium and unique blindness. A seeing blindness" (93).

What happens in mourning is images are left "in us." But all images, including ones of the self, are composed of the other, too: "I now inhabit the interiority of an image" (Lippit 95). Film is a medium that seems to create such a proliferation of ghosts. Blindness comes from the simple fact of being recorded. In *Echographies*, Derrida describes the death effect of the photography as a "night light" descending onto its subjects:

> It is a night visibility. As soon as there is a technology of the image, visibility brings night. It incarnates in a night body, it radiates a night light. At this moment, in this room, night is falling over us. Even if it weren't falling, we are already in night, as soon as we are captured by optical instruments which don't even need the light of day. We are already specters of a "televised." In the nocturnal space in which this image of us, this picture we are in the process of having "taken," is described, it is already night … Our disappearance is already here. (Derrida and Stiegler 115–117)

Where Lippit sees only darkness and a sense of losing oneself, Derrida might affirm the positive forces of inheritance as they relate to images, to say nothing for the multiplicity of others now inhabiting us. We are other, too: when the photograph is taken, and you're under the gaze of the lens, we are blind, but maybe hopeful about who might see us, or rather who we would like for us to be seen by—*I want to be seen looking even though I am blind*. Lippit argues that, in Derrida, life, spectrality, and autobiography all hinge around this theme of blindness. "Blindness, in Derrida's idiom, emerges less as the absence of vision, and more as the inability to see someone or something—who or what, ultimately myself—at a critical moment" (89). What is this critical moment? Later he writes, "[B]lindness is the mechanism or condition through which one sees oneself" (92). Autobiography must pass through blindness for a centred and "complete" picture of the self.

Is there then not an *impossibility* of the autobiography that is in fact generated by the spectres? Lippit argues, "Everything arrives in reflection, from an other to me. I am this subject, reflected; the subject of life, spectrality, and autobiography" (90). He continues,

> It haunts the present in advance, it haunts me in advance, which is to say that I always come before it, before the specter and the law of spectrality, which watches me. I am always in the scene of spectrality. (87)

Already regarding the other that remains unpredictable and unprogrammable as justice itself, the spectral gaze that brings Actor and Viewer together regards the actor in the biographical documentary. When we view the documentary, we are blinded in turn when the gaze of the other, through the subject's pose, regards us. Cinema is a blinding medium *par excellence*, but it does open up a space for the other. Lippit does not expand his theory of spectrality to make room for alterity and the productive forces of mourning, opting instead for something akin to a philosophical stalemate. If visual culture is full of spectres, then our identities, memories, and knowledge is also full of images that make us open to radical alterity, as Saghafi suggests.

Derrida relates his impression of the dominance of visual thinking and metaphors in philosophy: "What dominated Western logos, philosophy, Western discourse, Western culture, especially its philosophical form, was precisely sight, the metaphorical reference to the visual (*Penser* 71).⁵" In secret cinema, the self that sees is blind. The subject internalizes a non-seeing self. Each trace in Lippit is an encounter with an invisible visible—each instance of spectrality brings you closer to blindness. On the constellation of life, spectrality, and autobiography, Lippit writes,

> Vitality and spectral visuality, life and blindness, converge in Derrida's thought upon a subject always haunted by life and the specter, yielding always a spectral form of autobiography, a secret autobiography of the other. Secret and other because, the *biograph*, and especially the *autobiograph*, always comes to me from elsewhere, from the outside, from another, and remains in the end secret to me. (89–90)

We are confronted with a blind subject because the nature of writing and visuality is reflection. The spectre delays full, coherent meaning. As soon as we are photographed, we meld with the techne of medium and exist as a spectre from another time and place.

Lippit argues essentially there is no such thing as an auto-biography, because the trace of writing or filming is supplementary, never the origin, which creates new memories. Any autobiography will be a series of selections, representations, framings. Autobiography blinds the subject to the very subject matter at hand. Within the moment of the being filmed, it is impossible to recall the full picture, and yet it is presented as full, and fully transparent. In the biographical documentary we see blind subjects, participants who are being regarded and hence under a spectral gaze, subjects subject to the laws of delay. Saghafi explains spectrality as fundamentally about our responsibility toward the other, and thus not exclusively a Marxist notion, although Marxism is implied in this responsibility. Openness toward the other is a criterion of spectral logic. But responsibility expands the notion of blindness to something more, something ethical.

Derrida's interest lies in the process of cinema as opposed to the isolated study of an individual film text. Is it ex-cinema (Lippit)? It cannot be denied that all the threads pass through the knot of hospitality. The significance of the face in Levinas and Derrida's engagement with it will also be explored in the following chapter, but let us describe the basic dynamic of the face-to-face. Because the face of the other is often the first element that gets experienced in the face-to-face, it holds an especially strong position in the articulation of hospitality. No encounter with the other fails to include a third dimension, which is defined as the unseen dimension of Justice. Ethics is a kind of gaze that sees you but you don't see, residing most likely in a certain relation between at least two people that communicate only asymmetrically. Derrida explains, "The illeity of the third is nothing less, for Levinas, than the beginning of justice, at once as law and beyond the law" ("From Adieu à Emmanuel Levinas" 25). It is upon this moment of blindness that Derrida has tried to expand in his writings on the visible and visual arts, and in his very active collaborations with photographers and filmmakers, which is really a relationship he forms with the technologies of photography and cinema.

In "From Adieu à Emmanuel Levinas," an essay on hospitality, Derrida notes how Levinas' "Phenomenology of Eros" is turned toward the feminine and operates from

> a *point of view* that goes blindly (with no view [*point de vue*]) in this place of non-light that "The Feminine" would be insofar as it is "essentially violable and inviolable." This inviolable violability, this vulnerability of a being that prohibits violence at the very place it is exposed to it without defense, is what, in the feminine, seems to have the countenance of the face itself, even though the feminine "presents a face that goes beyond the face," there where *eros* "consists in going beyond the possible." (30)

A constellation of themes and concepts presents itself here: exposure, vulnerability, hospitality, the feminine, blindness. Derrida's terminology of hospitality that draws so heavily on Levinas actually parallels and overlaps with the terms he uses in his writings on photography, especially in *Copy, Archive, Signature* and a long essay on photography "Aletheia." The event called hospitality also shares important dimensions with spectrality, especially at those points of vulnerability and blindness. In a sense, what is more vulnerable than letting in ghosts, letting them do the talking and talking with them? In a sense, our relation to cinema is a way to play this out, to place belief in something that has no reason to exist, to be true—hauntology.

Jacques Derrida felt he was being tailed the entire time he was in Prague in late December 1981. As he relates in *Ghost Dance* in section 6 called "Trial. Power through absence," he felt he was under Kafka's gaze the entire time. The voice-over monologue plays over a storming sea. It is just one of many scenes in the film featuring the ocean. Derrida says,

> Last year, exactly a year ago, I went to Prague to take part in a private seminar with some dissident Czech philosophers who were banned from the universities. I was followed by the Czech secret police who made no secret about it. After the seminar I went for a walk round Kafka's town as if in pursuit of Kafka's ghost who was, in fact, himself pursuing me. I went to see the houses where Kafka lived ... there are two in Prague. And I went to his grave. I found out the next day when I was arrested for drug smuggling, supposedly, that it was at the exact time that I was at Kafka's grave, and so preoccupied to some extent with Kafka's ghost, that the Czech secret police entered my room and planted a little packet of drugs as a pretext for my arrest the next day. When I was interrogated by the police as to why I was in Prague, I answered truthfully that I was preparing a paper on Kafka on an extract from Kafka's "The Trial" called "Before the Court". And so throughout my short interrogation and imprisonment Kafka's ghost was effectively present. And Kafka's script was manipulating the whole scene, the scene being that of "The Trial," in a certain way, as if we were all acting in a film controlled by Kafka's ghost.

Pascale and Melanie sit on the boardwalk, having just killed their big oaf friend-turned-rapist in the previous scene. The film then cuts to traffic in the city at night, the "sea of electric eels." The two women are haunted but they don't say what they are haunted by, driving home the sense that, in postmodernity, dissemination of ghosts leads to a general haunting.

Through its uncanny status and potential appeal to presence (Derrida's presence through his voice), Derrida's voice-over replaces Kafka or at least meets up with Kafka as the origin of the Kafkaesque. The image replaced by voice puts the subject in a non-space, a space always to be determined, like a single boat on the rollicking ocean. Derrida's voice-over functions to detach the voice from the body; the authority loosens from the person but remains attached to the other. The voice travels through time, space, and others, me. All versions of "Before the Law" couldn't have been written without being haunted by Kafka which is another way of saying before the law of the name. For Derrida, the title is the thing that makes all literature (and not only that) before the law. In film, that may be the role of the face of the other, and rights around the ownership of one's own image that follow.

The Prague imprisonment was an intriguing event in his life specifically because he immediately wrote about the experience, and then a few years later in "Circumfession." He describes his first TV interview:

The very first time I spoke before a television camera, I had to be silent about what *my* experience was, which at that moment didn't hold any great interest. It was at night, in Germany, on the train that brought me back from Prague. It seemed to me that, at that moment, I ought to speak of what had just happened, to which I was the only one capable of testifying and which had some general interest. Still I had to be satisfied with broad stereotypes ... (*Points* 129)

He doesn't say whether those limitations of the first interview on the event were self-imposed or not, but one can guess that a major television news network would not have broadcast a deconstructive analysis of a news story.

Blindness's call to embrace the other was put to the test for Derrida with the Prague imprisonment affair. Importantly, he associates all the photographs that were taken of him during this affair with nakedness: "I have never been more photographed in my life, from the airport to the prison, clothed or naked before putting on the prisoner's 'uniform'" (*Points* 128–129). Derrida would repeat this scene of imprisonment in film and would thus open up new voices while being blinded anew, living the "spectral life." In *Ghost Dance, D'ailleurs, Derrida*, and in *Derrida*, the Prague imprisonment gets retold. It is not a coincidence that Derrida chose a blinding medium like cinema to re-iterate this scene: "I love repetition, as if the future were entrusted to us, as if it were waiting for us in the cipher of a very ancient speech—one which has not yet been allowed to speak" (*Points* 130). To keep the law alive, repetition or delay or desire must play a role in the scene. By repeating this scene, which is, for Derrida, associated with his first TV appearance, meant a way of letting new voices in, altering the meaning, expanding it, and, finally, letting it differ indefinitely, as if he was, with every new iteration, "before the law." The scene in *Before the Law*, as in the Prague incarceration, also makes possible a certain blurring of both fiction and non-fiction, as evinced in the poetic moments in *Ghost Dance* and *D'ailleurs, Derrida*.

Derrida was brought to Czechoslovakia by a group of intellectuals for a series of conferences on philosophy. Day and night, he sensed he was being followed. At the airport, on the return home, officers—*possibly*—pretended to find four bags containing drugs in his luggage. He was driven to the police station and interrogated for six to seven hours. His requests to speak to French authorities were denied. At midnight, he was imprisoned. Here, he stresses the brutal treatment that he had to undergo. The guards sarcastically rejected all his demands to speak to lawyers, the French ambassador, and even for a translator. The Czech authorities said it was highly unlikely that he had no knowledge of the drugs that were planted on him. Drug smugglers are often people that you would least suspect, like intellectuals or singers, they told him. He was brutally thrown into a dungeon and the door was shut. He had to wear a specific uniform. The next night, they released him. In the meantime, he had no idea what was going on outside the dungeon, and he was told that if found guilty, the trial could last, after a two-month period, an unlimited time and that the penalty would be two years in prison. He ends the interview with a salute to those Czech intellectuals who fight for human rights in properly heroic conditions, that is to say, obscure and anonymous.

The Prague imprisonment reoccurs no less than four times in Derrida's screen performances. A TV news interview from 2 January 1982, in *Ghost Dance*, and in both documentaries.[6] Every new retelling of the event is both general and singular. He writes, "Every sign can break with every given context and engender infinitely new contexts in an absolutely nonsaturable fashion" (*Margins* 320). "According to several of his friends, images of Prague would come back to him for months: he would regularly have the feeling that people were following him, eavesdropping, or hunting him down," (339) Peeters explains.

Antenne 2 aired interviews with friends and colleagues greeting him at the station. On his arrival at the airport, Peeters via Marguerite Derrida relates,

> [He] hardly had time to say hello. He left with Marguerite and Jean [his son] for the studio of Antenne 2 to view, with the journalist, the interview that had been filmed in the train: it was a delicate matter and he was anxious not to compromise anyone by a clumsy phrase. (338)

In the TV interview, he doesn't mention Kafka even though he plays a starring role in its retelling in "Before the Law" and *Ghost Dance*. Peeters claims, "This arrest brought him centre stage, without his having asked for it. But it was without the least doubt one of the things that led him to *lay himself open* more and more, especially in the political arena" (341). The incident certainly seemed to go hand-in-hand with revoking his self-imposed ban on his public image.

Derrida knew that what something like the Prague affair actually called for was embracing multiple voices and a heterogeneity of discourses. Derrida states,

> A single voice on the line, a continuous speech, that is what they want to impose. This authoritarian norm would be like an unconscious plot, an intrigue of the hierarchies (ontological, theologico-political, technico-metaphysic), the very ones that call for deconstructive analyses. (*Points* 130)

Could Derrida really conduct a psychoanalytical session on hospitality in a 7-minute news interview when the interviewer just wants the concrete facts? There is a sense that Derrida always regretted this initial interview on Channel 2. He imagines developing a commentary on the state of human rights "today," the political question of the subject, inventing new narrative forms to articulate the event, and expressing his regret that he had to leave his cellmates. Derrida states,

Just imagine the look on the faces of the reporters and the TV viewers. But the diffi-culty I felt in the most acute way at that moment is permanent, and it is what para-lyzes me every time I have to take the floor and speak in public. Even here, still now. (*Points* 129)

He would need to incorporate new and different voices to redeploy the story, to get it right once but not for all.

On the fictional aspects of Kafka's story "Before the Law," Derrida writes, "The structure of this event is such that one is compelled neither to believe nor disbelieve it. Like the question of belief, that of the reality of its historical referent is, if not annulled, at least irremediably fissured" (199). Our relationship toward the Law is out of necessity a blind and spectral one. Describing the murder of the father who keeps haunting his children in Freud's *Totem and Taboo*, Derrida main-tains the logic of spectrality revolves around the question of belief:

> The structure of this event is such that one is compelled neither to believe nor disbe-lieve it. Like the question of belief, that of the reality of its historical referent is, if not annulled, at least irremediably fissured. Demanding and denying the story, this qua-si-event bears the mark of fictive narrativity ... Whether or not it is fantastic, whether or not it has arisen from the imagination, even the transcendental imagination, and whether it states or silences the origin of the fantasy, this in no way diminishes the imperious necessity of what it tells, its law. This law is even more frightening and fantastic, *unheimlich* or uncanny, that if it emanated from pure reason ... ("Before the Law" 199)

This Law does not speak from the terrain of the living or the actual.

Derrida stays loyal to the structure of Kafka's text in all his retellings of what he calls the "Prague Affair" in *Counterpath*. The respect before the law, or before the text, finds a corollary in film and photography, as spectrality propels respect for the other photographed that can't be assimilated, only repeated, translated, loyally. Retelling the story keeps more than a literary text alive, but enters into a relation with the Law itself. Kafka's story about the man from the country and the guard who both stand before the law offers Derrida not only an opportunity to reflect on the legal, that is non-literary, aspect of literature, but the very structure of the Law: "The only two characters in the story are blind and separated from one another, and from the law. Such is the modality of this rapport, of this relation, of this narration: blindness and separation, a kind of non-rapport" ("Before the Law" 201–202). Derrida often writes as if he were the man from the country, the man "before the law":

> I thought that at last, at last, I was going to be able to rehearse, and then write, write for years in pencil on a clean whitewood political prisoners' table, I see the film of

my whole life …[O]ut of school and into prison, that's what I return to every day, that's what I'm becoming, that's what I was, that's where I write, each time caught up again by one and freed from the other, more locked up in one than in the other, but which, each time from the feeling of an illegible accident, of a wound as virtual … (Bennington and Derrida 292–293)

On the theme of blindness in *D'ailleurs, Derrida*, he writes,

What I have noted at the moment, for the blind man (a figure among others but that stands in for all of them—for the Actor, for the Spectator, for the film, even maybe for the Operators, for the Author, for the Editor, etc.) we could relate it to other metonymies of the films. […] It is the metonymy of all metonymies, the very game that the film plays. (Derrida and Fathy 82)[7]

Still blind, haunted by a law that requires him to repeat the same scene—could this be Derrida's ultimate secret trauma in *Derrida*?—Derrida repeats this event not only to raise awareness of the spectral "wrong man," and to proclaim his survival, but because it is a scene that has left him with the sense of being watched by the other.[8] For him, documentary filmmaking creates a self open to radical alterity: "How do you want me to be, and do you want me to be myself? I could make many more films *and* with other material. […] I would always be 'me,' certainly, but each time another" (Derrida and Fathy 79).[9]

In "Circumfession," he even leaves open the possibility of guilt or non-innocence as he relates the event to his childhood expulsion from school:

Whether they expelled me or threw me into prison, I always thought the other must have good reason to accuse me. I did not see, I did not even see my eyes, any more than in the past I saw the hand raising the knife above me …[K]now that I am dying of shame, but of a shame in which I persevere all the more in that I have nothing to do with it, I'm not admitting anything and yet I am ready to justify or even repeat the very thing I'm being accused of. (Bennington and Derrida 300, 302)

This is how Derrida works through the event: by repeating it, conjuring it, he erects a law and a promise from it, from blindness (and fiction). Haunted by a self who has already been ready to die for his convictions, Derrida settles in comfortably to his sentence of repeating this circumcision-like operation of sending out new versions of his spectral self. This blindness before the law is at once highly productive and intolerable.

In the film, he walks through a Spanish desert while his voice-over monologue speaks of hospitality:

I have experienced what could be called the opposite of hospitality from the country and the police who arrested me and from the prison guards who threatened to hit me, etc. It's the opposite of hospitality, and yet, in the prison itself, despite the brevity of my stay there, I did have two experiences of true hospitality, memories that I hold very dear.

He enters abandoned houses, as if entering a nightmare, without sight. As he enters, exits, and re-enters the Spanish ruins, he goes from naturally lit to phantom silhouette.

The film cuts to flowers in the desert when he turns to the "two experiences of hospitality." This portion of the film is done in talking head interview style with Derrida sitting near a rocky background saying,

> I was jailed at one in the morning and at five or six, they threw another prisoner into the cell. A gypsy, a Hungarian Tzigane, with whom I immediately struck up an intense friendship for several hours. He initiated me into a certain number of things, offering to wash the walls, because we had to wash the walls. We had to do a certain number of things the guards told us to do. So, to cut a long story short, for the few hours I spent with this man in this little prison, I had an experience of friendship and hospitality such that, in that little cell, this man, who knew prison better than me, welcomed me.

Then he smiles ecstatically:

> I began to dream that this prison would be hospitable to me. And then, despite the violence, the suffering—because it was an extremely cruel interlude—there was something in me ...—I may have mentioned this somewhere, I don't remember where— something in me that rehearsed this scene, that lived this scene as a rehearsal. As if I had desired it, as if I had anticipated it, as if I let myself be drawn along by something which had already happened that I was beginning again. And this rehearsal was like a certain desire that stemmed from hospitality. I was welcomed in a place that was already prepared within me. As if I had done everything to get myself locked up. When you reconstruct the chain of events that led me to that prison, I had done everything foolish I needed to do to get arrested and thrown in prison. And so there is a rehearsal, where there is a mixture of torture, of suffering—I won't go into that—but also of delight. Delight because of the rehearsal.

Now he walks in the desert while he finishes the monologue in voice-over: "There was someone in me who said, that's good, this only happens to me and I recognize it. I find a certain psychic accommodation, a certain expectation. In a way, I was waiting for it." Shots of the abandoned dwellings end the sequence. This sequence introduces yet another ghost into the mix: the gypsy becomes a powerful force in the scene of a violent law. As such, the person Derrida feels most hospitality from—the one that permits all—who welcomes him the most wholly becomes the new author of the event.

No single version of the Prague imprisonment is more noteworthy than any other, even when it is ostensibly reduced to a simple anecdote in *Derrida* (2002): "He is arrested and thrown in prison for 24 hours in Prague for transporting drugs, which the authorities plant on him." But the fact that it reappears throughout these filmed appearances suggests it gives us something to think in relation to his overall work on spectrality and cinema. How do we inherit the responsibility that Derrida locates in his incarceration? This moment of surveillance is a political warning in the Kafkaesque sense of being seen and blinded before the other. "I promise you, you will be haunted, too," it seems to say. Imprisonment can ostensibly haunt us in ways other than the intentions of the guards. That's why we can laugh, find humour, and find hospitality in it. Hospitality is after all a moment of freedom and survival. Imprisonment is an experience like photography, which produces a sense of the self as a ghost, in an almost visceral way. The film retellings could be a way of changing the ghosts that haunt that scene: from fear and anguish in the first television version to openness toward the other in *D'ailleurs, Derrida*, where the place and time of the event are not even named. Forever blinded, Derrida replays the scene, re-enacts it, indefinitely, accommodating the other.

Another Derrida always already haunts this scene: from the past or the future, Derrida seeks to alter the brutality and inhospitality that would seem to fully characterize this scene. Finding the hospitable in the inhospitable was Derrida's answer to the brutality of the event, his way of offering another law found in the gaze of the other. Once again, he remains before the law. Ironically, the Czech authorities never cleared the charges against him (Peeters 339). Derrida stresses the political and legal responsibility to talk to the ghost, to inhabit its scene, its play, because it is only there that responsibility to the other is born. Indeed, it is only within spectrality that you become unconditionally hospitable. By turning the Prague incident into a motif in his film work, it suggests he sees this event already as a kind of literary scene, like a scene out of Kafka, and not only a literary scene but one where visibility, nakedness, invisibility play roles, in short, a cinematic scene. Being a scene of blindness, where Derrida's blindness is projected it would seem, the closest thing to it, the only way for him to re-live, re-play it would perhaps be in cinema. But when the scene of blindness is projected, it in turn blinds the viewer, putting the viewer before the law. This chapter has begun to explore how the most interesting asymmetrical communication of this scene has perhaps been between Derrida's multiple spectral selves.

Notes

1. More recently, *Facs of Life* (dir. Maglioni and Thomson, France/Italy/UK, 2009) creates experimental montage sequences using archive footage of another postmodernist philosopher, Gilles Deleuze, to ask similar questions raised in the Derrida documentaries.

2. Egyptian-born filmmaker and scholar Fathy began her filmmaking career with short films about Arab culture and identity politics. *Hidden Faces* (1990), a portrait of Egyptian feminist Nawal Al Saadawi, took as its main topic the experience of women who break from tradition. Her second film, *Ghazeia* (1993), is about two belly dancers and sexual cultural politics. She writes, "I like putting a familiar subject in a new context so that it raises questions. In film you can show contradictory aspects of a character ... I don't think identity exists independently; it exists only in relation to others. My identity in France is different from the one I have in Egypt. There is obviously the core, the essence, which defines you as a person everywhere. But I'm different in Egypt, I'm different in France, I'm different in Germany ... In my filmmaking I was trying to integrate these different aspects into one. This means that people in Egypt can see the side of me that is not Egyptian, and people in France can see the side of me that is not French, not European. It's like collecting pieces and making yourself one person. It is not so easy, because the image I receive from other people is not exactly what I put out. The image also reflects how they see me" (Hillauer 74–75).

3. "Parler de perspectivisme, c'est dire qu'on voit toujours les choses, on interprète toujours les choses d'un certain point de vue, selon un intérêt, en découpant un schema de vision organisée, hiérarchisée, un schéma toujours sélectif qui, par conséquent, doit autant à l'aveuglement qu'à la vision."

4. "[N]ous ne les voyons pas *simultanément* comme voyants *et* visibles. [...] Dans l'expérience du miroir, cette indécision affleure. Quand nous nous regardons dans un miroir, nous devons choisir entre regarder la couleur de nos yeux et regarder le flux, l'influx du regard qui se regarde avec tous les paradoxes de l'autoportrait."

5. "[C]e qui dominait le logos occidental, la philosophie, les discours occidentaux, la culture occidentale, notamment sa forme philosophique, c'était précisément la vue, la référence au moins métaphorique au visuel."

6. Laure Adler also asks him to go over the events in the 1996 *Cercle de minuit* interview.

7. "Ce que je remarque à l'instant pour l'aveugle (figure entre autres mais qui vaut *une fois pour toutes*—pour l'Acteur, pour le Spectateur, pour le Film, peut-être même pour les Opérateurs et pour l'Auteur, pour le Monteur ou la Monteuse, etc.), nous pourrions le rapporter à d'autres métonymies du film. [...] Elle est la métonymie des métonymies, le jeu même du film."

8. On the theme of survival in his work, Derrida insists, "[D]econstruction is always on the side of the *yes*, on the side of the affirmation of life. Everything I say—at least from '*Pas*' (in *Parages*) on—about survival as a complication of the opposition life/death proceeds in me from an unconditional affirmation of life. This surviving is life beyond life, life more than life, and my discourse is not a discourse of death, but, on the contrary, the affirmation of a living being who prefers living and thus surviving to death, because survival is not simply that which remains but the most intense life possible" (*Learning to Live Finally* 51–52).

9. "Comment voulez-vous que je sois, et que je sois moi-même? Je pourais l'être de tant d'autres façons, on pourrait faire tant d'autres films, *et* avec un autre matériau. [...] [J]'y serais toujours 'moi', certes, mais chaque fois un autre."

Bibliography

Achbar, Mark, and Peter Wintonick, dirs. *Manufacturing Consent: Noam Chomsky and the Media*. 1992. DVD. Zeitgeist Video, 2002.

Altman, Rick. "Television/Sound." *Studies in Entertainment: Critical Approaches to Mass Culture.* Ed. Tania Modleski. Bloomington: Indiana University Press, 1986. 39–54.

Barthes, Roland. *Mythologies.* Trans. Annette Lavers. New York: Hill and Wang, 1972.

———. *Camera Lucida: Reflections on Photography.* Trans. Richard Howard. York: Hill and Wang, 1981.

Benjamin, Walter. *The Work of Art in the Age of Its Technological Reproducibility and Other Writings on Media.* Ed. Michael W. Jennings, Brigid Doherty, Thomas Y. Levin. Cambridge, MA: Belknap Press of Harvard University Press, 2008.

Bennington, Geoffrey, and Jacques Derrida. *Jacques Derrida.* Trans. Geoffrey Bennington. Chicago, IL: University of Chicago Press, 1993.

Chaplin, Tamara. *Turning on the Mind: French Philosophers on Television.* Chicago, IL: University of Chicago Press, 2007.

Deleuze, Gilles, and Félix Guattari. *What Is Philosophy?* Trans. Hugh Tomlinson and Graham Burchell. New York: Columbia University Press, 1994.

Derrida, Jacques. *Dissemination.* Trans. Barbara Johnson. Chicago, IL: University of Chicago Press, 1981.

———. *Margins of Philosophy.* Trans. Alan Bass. Chicago, IL: University of Chicago Press, 1982.

———. *The Post Card: From Socrates to Freud and Beyond.* Trans. Alan Bass. Chicago and London: University of Chicago Press, 1987a.

———. *The Truth in Painting.* Trans. Geoff Bennington and Ian McLeod. Chicago, IL: University of Chicago Press, 1987b.

———. "Before the Law." *Acts of Literature.* Ed. Derek Attridge. New York: Routledge, 1992.

———. *Memoirs of the Blind: The Self-Portrait and Other Ruins.* Trans. Pascale-Anne Brault and Michael Naas. Chicago, IL: University of Chicago Press, 1993.

———. *Points …: Interviews, 1974–1994.* Ed. Elisabeth Weber. Stanford, CA: Stanford University Press, 1995.

———. Interview with Laure Adler. *Le cercle de minuit.* France 2. Paris. 23 April 1996.

———. "From Adieu à Emmanuel Levinas." *Research in Phenomenology* 28.1 (1998): 20–36.

———. *Who's Afraid of Philosophy: Right to Philosophy 1.* Trans. Jan Plug. Stanford, CA: Stanford University Press, 2002.

———. *Learning to Live Finally: The Last Interview.* Trans. Pascale-Anne Brault and Michael Naas. Hoboken, NJ: Melville House Publishing, 2007.

———. *Copy, Archive, Signature: A Conversation on Photography.* Trans. Jeff Fort. Stanford, CA: Stanford University Press, 2010.

———. *Penser à ne pas voir: Écrits sur les arts du visible 1979–2004.* Paris: Éditions de la différence, 2013.

Derrida, Jacques, and Bernard Stiegler. *Echographies of Television.* Trans. Jennifer Bajorek. Cambridge: Polity Press, 2002.

Derrida, Jacques, and Catherine Malabou. *Counterpath: Traveling with Jacques Derrida.* Trans. David Wills. Stanford, CA: Stanford University Press, 2004.

Derrida, Jacques, and Marie-François Plissart. *Right of Inspection*. Trans. David Wills. New York: Monacelli Press, 1998.

Derrida, Jacques, and Safaa Fathy. *Tourner les mots: au bord d'un film*. Paris: Éditions Galilée, 2000.

Dick, Kirby, and Amy Ziering Kofman, dirs. *Derrida*. 2002. DVD. Zeitgeist Video, 2003.

———, eds. *Derrida: Screenplay and Essays on the Film Derrida*. Manchester: Manchester University Press, 2005.

Doane, Mary Ann. "The Voice in the Cinema: The Articulation of Body and Space." *Film Theory and Criticism: Introductory Readings*. 5th ed. Ed. Leo Braudy and Marshall Cohen. New York and Oxford: Oxford University Press, 1999. 363–375.

Fargier, Jean-Paul, dir. *Mémoires d'aveugle: Le film de l'exposition*. 1990. VHS. Editions du Seuil/ Réunion des Musées Nationaux, 1992.

Fathy, Safaa, dir. *D'Ailleurs, Derrida*. 2000. DVD. Éditions Montparnasse, 2008.

Foucault, Michel. "Two Lectures." *Power/Knowledge: Selected Interviews & Others Writings 1972–1977*. Ed. Colin Gordon. New York: Pantheon Books, 1977.

———. "What Is an Author?" *The Foucault Reader*. Ed. Paul Rabinow. New York: Pantheon Books, 1984.

Frank, Marcie. *How to Be an Intellectual in the Age of TV: The Lessons of Gore Vidal*. Durham, NC: Duke University Press, 2005.

Hillauer, Rebecca. *Encyclopedia of Arab Women Filmmakers*. Trans. Allison Brown, Deborah Cohen, and Nancy Joyce. Cairo and New York: The American University in Cairo Press, 2005.

Jousse, Thierry. "A propos d'un abécédaire." *Cahiers du cinéma* 510 (Février 1997): 20–21.

Lamont, Michèle. "How to Become a Dominant French Philosopher: The Case of Jacques Derrida." *American Journal of Sociology* 93.3 (1987): 584–622.

Lippit, Akira Mizuta. *Ex-Cinema: From a Theory of Experimental Film and Video*. Berkeley: University of California Press, 2012.

Maglioni, Silvia, and Graeme Thomson, dirs. *Facs of Life*. 2009. DOC Alliance Films. 24 February 2020. http://dafilms.com/film/7899-facs-of-life/.

McMullen, Ken, dir. *Ghost Dance*. 1983. DVD. Mediabox, 2006.

Peeters, Benoît. *Derrida: A Biography*. Trans. Andrew Brown. Cambridge, UK: Polity Press, 2013.

Shumway, David R. "The Star System in Literary Studies." *PMLA* 112.1 (January 1997): 85–100.

Taylor, Astra, dir. *Žižek!* 2005. DVD. Zeitgeist Films, 2005.

CHAPTER FIVE

4ᵗʰ *Séance*: Cinécircumcision: Phantom Parts in the Archive

A turn toward New Historicism has marked recent documentary filmmaking practises. The sense of discovery and surprise that now often occurs at the moment of reception in visual culture results from our finding new meaning in old images. Temporal and contextual disparity gives these modern artifacts an archive effect (Baron, *Archive Effect*). Extending on this argument, I argue spectrality is an important element of the archive effect in terms of how it creates a desire to engage (communicate with and mourn) the other. By focusing on performances that counter-sign authorial intention in documentary film, I aim to elucidate both temporal and intentional aspects of spectrality. The ghostly characters' *aliveness* suggests a contact with the historical past, often through eyeline, gaze, and other forms of bodily presence and contact. Authorial disparity or a challenge to authors' intentions can be seen in the interview segments and the general "cat and mouse game" happening in *Derrida* (2002). Other films like *Sans soleil* (1983) and *Grizzly Man* (2005) also emphasize the relationship between the other's gaze and the inauguration of the archive. Archive fever and spectrality relate to the analysis of documentary film and how this genre has become a way of experiencing the past afresh through old footage.

Jaimie Baron has recently showed how documentary film is marked by what she calls an "archive effect," suggesting New Historicist epistemologies have directly or indirectly influenced documentary filmmaking: "That is, they generate and maintain a productive tension between the description of the specificity of a given cultural and historical situation and an interrogation of textuality itself" ("Contemporary Documentary" 15). Films of course have a special relation to the archiving impulse: "Film theorist Mary Ann Doane, following Kittler, has suggested that the ability of technologies of mechanical reproduction to create indexical traces holds both the allure of the preservation of the past and the threat of preserving too much, of generating only an 'archive of noise'" ("Contemporary Documentary" 17). But what one theorist calls "noise" another will call meaningful in the future.

In *Archive Effect*, Baron explains at length how temporality and intentional disparity pave ways for new understandings of the pre-existing footage. Films like the *Up* series (dir. Apted, UK, 1964–2012), *A Film Unfinished* (dir. Hersonski, GR/IL, 2010), *Tearoom* (US, 1962/2007) rely on the archive effect. On *Tearoom*, Baron writes, "While there is also certainly a difference between 1962 (the year in which the footage was made) and 2007 (the year in which Tearoom was 'made'), there is also, unavoidably, its sameness" (*Archive* 44–45). Baron adds,

> If we think of the archive effect as potentially ambiguous experience in which multiple meanings for the same document may coexist simultaneously, we may also be able to better acknowledge both the ruptures and the continuities between 'our' and the 'other' historical and social contexts presented to us in archival documents as they are constituted as such in appropriation films. (*Archive* 45)

The fact remains that temporal disparity—the way we read footage differently over time—is always possible immediately after the footage is produced. To attend to the various interpretations of the footage is the job of the historian. The textual elements of such films suggest a level of self-conscious play with notions of history and archive. The films do the heavy lifting in other words vis-à-vis the New Historicist and deconstructive epistemological approaches that drive them.

The New Historicist tendency in documentary includes a number of characteristics including divergent discourses, satire and irony, and "a move away from the 'transfer of meaning,' or the attempt to narrate and explain history, toward a 'transfer of presence,' or a sense of contact with the historical past that cannot be reduced to facts and chronologies," ("Contemporary Documentary" 14) according to Baron. On Rebecca Baron's *okay bye-bye* (1999), Baron continues, "[T]he film fragment that sets off the narrative is ultimately unassimilable to narrative; its meaning is left open and unresolved" ("Contemporary Documentary" 21). The reality is now what finds its way into the digital archive depends on who finds what images and chooses to make them available. There is always an excess of the archive—what the archive cannot contain. This uncanny fragment is understood by Baron as the "metonym rather than the metaphor that offers the comic or tragic release from the satire of meaning(lessness) in the form of a transfer of *presence* of history, rather than its meaning, to the viewer" ("Contemporary Documentary" 23).

Baron's point is the "archive effect" creates presence only on condition of what she calls temporal disparity: "[W]hat makes footage read as 'archival' is, first of all, the effect within a given film generated by the juxtaposition of shots perceived as produced at different moments in time" (*Archive* 17). The *Up* series' main strategy is in fact juxtaposing footage of its subjects at different ages/stages in their lives. Although Derrida would critique the "real-time" effect and artifactuality of modern teletechnology as types of logocentric presence where disparity is minimized, spectral communication registers a more complex relation to the image, one which oscillates between two poles: spectres are both present and absent at the same time. Their temporality disobeys all rules, *coming back* unexpectedly, returning to watch over us. Baron describes the archival quality of today's visual culture:

> While the sheer volume of recorded—and digitized—audiovisual documents now multiplies every day, this promise of 'rare' archival footage continues to exercise an epistemological seduction and to feed the desire for a revelatory truth about the past that, of course, can never be fully satisfied. (*Archive* 6–7)

Baron's ironic search for aura connects with effects of the cinematic archive and Derridean spectrality.

Often regarded as a philosopher of purely postmodern literary and linguistic effects, uninterested in the life of the body (Burt; Strathausen), Derrida actually began and ended his philosophical body of work on questions of auto-affection, self-presence, voice, that is, issues directly related to the living body. In *On Touching, Jacques Derrida, Echographies of Television*, and the films, *Ghost Dance* (1983), *D'ailleurs, Derrida* (1999), and *Derrida*, the cinematic body part allows Derrida to confront the "violence of exappropriation." The transfer of Derrida's body parts from philosophy into cinema and then back again to philosophy has meant that the question of the body of the philosopher has become essential in recent scholarship. In Akira Mizuta Lippit, Nicholas Royle, Laurence Simmons, and others, the cinematic bodily presence of Derrida has been a source for philosophy. *How do Derrida's body fragments return to him? What is the stronger ghostly presence: Derrida's voice or his gaze?* if such questions can be posed at all. As the multiple edits and extras on the *Derrida* DVD would suggest, the released version of the film was just one of multiple possible versions. In one deleted scene that focuses on Derrida's body parts, Ziering Kofman, the film's director, explains how she at one time envisioned a film composed completely devoid of the philosopher's face:

> Early on I said to Jacques, and I wasn't kidding, that maybe Jacques wouldn't even appear in the film and I was trying to get away from this author-centered thing and it would just be body parts. And so I instructed Kirsten [Johnson] just to shoot his feet, his hands, that we would have something to work with if we ever wanted to go in that direction.

Circumcision frames Derrida, but it's a secretive framework. Circumcision appears at the beginning of a career of writing and then re-emerges at the end through his work in film. It's almost as if through his late work in film and on film Derrida found a way to continue expanding on circumcision. Other salient uses of the circumcision metaphor abound in his writings. In "Faith and Knowledge," "Schiboleth," and throughout "Circumfession," he develops the aporia and consequences of the event itself, and some scholars argue circumcision is Derrida's only true alliance, the origin, if you will, of his philosophical identity (Baum). But it is in his elaboration of the metaphor vis-à-vis cinema, I argue, where he finds a direct corollary with circumcision's uses and disuses of *his own* body proper. For Derrida, cinema was like writing because of its ability to create traces that could part—*parts du corps*. Never had he experienced the powerful spectralization of a presence within absence until he took part in cinema and photography, and started to grapple with the effects and ethics of telecommunication in *Specters of Marx, Echographies of Television*, and beyond. It was only within his late period that Derrida could have made the radical politics of circumcision prominent.

Derrida invites scrutiny. It stands to reason that he encouraged this slicing and splicing of his body parts and their critical examination by scholars eager to know more about circumcision's impact. In his notebooks for his grand book on circumcision that he started but could never finish, Derrida writes,

> *Circumcision, that's all I've ever talked about, consider the discourse on the limit, margins, marks, marches, etc., the closure, the ring (alliance and gift), the sacrifice, the writing of the body, the* pharmakos *excluded or cut off, the cutting/sewing of* Glas, *the blow and the sewing back up* ... (Bennington and Derrida 70)

And later, he compares it to a screen, albeit a spectral one emanating from a mark. The logic of circumcision is such that whatever it slices off can be grafted to something completely other, like in the Hegel half of *Glas*.

In *Jacques Derrida*, Geoffrey Bennington circles around the body of deconstruction. Never quoting Derrida literally, but only summarizing and appropriating the philosophy, "Derridabase" gives way to multiple entry points. He circumcises Derrida, giving deconstruction a future that can practically go on without him:

> [Bennington] has decided, by this rigorous circumcision, to do without my body, the body of my writings to produce basically, the 'logic' or the 'grammar,' the law of

production of every past, present, and why not future statement that I might have signed …[H]ere I am deprived of a future, no more event to come from me. (29–30)

Derrida can't reappropriate himself from Bennington. Every autobiography is a radical exappropriation where the self returns as other, a public archive, more naked and exposed. As Bennington slices away, Derrida senses almost nothing, but a part of him dies, unless he becomes unpredictable and quick.

The structure and principle of the archive rests upon spectrality. The suspense of spectrality gives the archive its power as well as its openness to the future: "The intensity of this suspension is vertiginous—and it gives vertigo while giving the only condition on which the future to come remains what it is: it is to come" (*Archive* 71–72). Derrida asks, "Is there a historian of the promise?" (*Archive* 70). As the archive both preserves and destroys content, the thing that the trace or cut stands in for remains unknown and unpredictable. Circumcision (branding, "printing," he writes in *Archive Fever*) is an induction into a culture, society, the world of language; it rounds up the individual into a race, but it simultaneously erects a secret, a history plagued by forgetting. Circumcision is a promise and a secret.

Like the archive, cinema preserves the still half living piece of the body: "The film is an art of cutting … of interruption that nevertheless lets live … We know very well that it all comes back to the art of montage, to the art of the edition, of editing in the English sense" (*Penser* 95).[1] Cinema's delicate operation of slicing and splicing parts of a subject doesn't go so far as to destroy or disfigure, but in creating another version of the self that can take on an afterlife of its own.

In "Le cinéma et ses fantômes," Derrida describes the experience of making *D'ailleurs, Derrida* (France), a 1999 biographical documentary by Safaa Fathy:

> Beyond everything I was able to indirectly learn, understand or come into proximity with the cinema, nothing was worth this inflexible experience that lets little retreat of the body. I was able to learn many things about cinema in general, about technology, about the market … In this sense, it was a "training film." (82)[2]

This film brings to the fore one of the subtlest specificities of cinematic *techne*: the way it attaches itself to the body (this time, of the philosopher). Fathy, an Arab feminist filmmaker, explores the way language, speech, the environment, and the apparatus itself become one with the body, and vice versa. There is no longer an abstract, universalizing discourse with cinema—rather, it is tied to the individual body. Derrida asks an important question about the body's relation to cinema: "And how to film words that become images, that are inseparable from the body, not only of the person that says them but of the body, the iconic assemblage, and that nevertheless preserves their sonority, their tone, their temporality?" (*Penser* 327).[3]

In a late talk on his experiences making *D'ailleurs, Derrida*—published as "Trace et archive, image et art"—Derrida suggests the autobiographic archive results in a complex interchange of parts of the self and parts of film. Traces or parts disseminate after the person is filmed. These traces or images are not simply objects, for Derrida, but forms of desire and intentionality (*Penser* 107). No image that has cut itself from the body proper is totally without a presence of its *own*. He writes,

> The film says to me: "You cannot reappropriate this thing here. The idiom, your absolute idiom, what you are, what you think, what you've said since the first circumcision, everything that is your idiom, which is the absolute proper, well, that proper appears to the other therefore is not reappropriable, you cannot reappropriate your own proper, your proper belongs to the other." (*Penser* 94)[4]

Derrida then briefly develops the double meaning of the word *part* in French:

> The film says, in French and English, it is naturally a part of me, undeniably, this idiom that I cannot reappropriate and that the film shows me, returns back to me, but also leaves me … I can die at any moment, the trace remains. The cut is there. It is a part of me that is cut from me and that therefore departs: it precedes, it emanates from me, but at the same time in separating, in cutting, and in detaching from me. And therefore, this part of me, I acquire it narcissistically, but I lose it at the same time. (*Penser* 105)[5]

The "proper" in logocentric thought is defined as a wholeness as well as a full presence that would claim to know, have a grip on, the self's understanding of the complete and intact body whose borders can be clearly drawn. In deconstruction, body parts, speaking parts, *greffes*, phantom parts return to the self after the spacialization and temporalization of the trace.

D'ailleurs, Derrida creates a montage of Derrida speaking about his life and philosophy with Paris, California, Algeria, and Spain as the backdrop. It is worth noting the original plan for the film included many additional elements than what appears in the final version. The director's "Note d'intention" suggests the film was conceived as a much more standard, less experimental documentary presenting Derrida's main philosophical points and making a case for the relevance of deconstruction today. Originally, for example, the film would put words on the screen that would form conceptual dualities: "Fully spelled out on the screen first in upper case is SPEECH and then in lower case is *writing*; likewise: SOUL *body*, INSIDE *outside*, MASCULINE *féminine*, PRESENCE *absence*, SENSIBLE *intelligible*, etc." (Fathy, "Note").[6] Jean-Luc Nancy would then offer a quick, handy definition of deconstruction: "Deconstruction comes down to presenting firstly what in metaphysics is called secondary as primary" (Fathy, "Note").[7] The image of the words would tremble and fall apart before reforming into new words: "On the screen we see that the letters becoming too unstable fall from their place and mix together" (Fathy, "Note").[8] The biographical or "life" aspects of Derrida are downplayed in the original version. What emerges thus in the finished film is a balance between the work and life aspects, which pose their own particular set of reading possibilities and conceptual knots.

In *D'ailleurs, Derrida*, he reads excerpts from "Circumfession" on camera. The finished film avoids presenting information in a pedagogical way. Instead it lets the themes emerge much more poetically through associations and through Derrida's own presence on film. In one sequence, we see Derrida typing away at the typewriter, the pages he has written, and he drops an envelope in a mailbox. Then the montage cuts to a young Derrida with dark hair and olive skin, placing the previous shots in an intellectual relation to the final one, creating an archive effect. The film then cuts to a scene where a photographer shoots Derrida. He says, "She takes photos, but it's not photography, it's hypnosis. Generally, taking a photo takes two or three seconds, this can take a minute. It's interminable. I don't know what to do." Derrida biographer Peeters writes, "Derrida participated more or less graciously in the productions that were proposed to him. He often seemed ill at ease and a bit wooden" (489). It is true in many scenes Derrida is seen passing by the camera, looking directly into the lens like a deer caught in the headlights. Fathy describes Derrida's interview style throughout the shoot as "a discourse of economy and nonexcess" (Derrida and Fathy 142).[9] Even during production, the eyeline is ostensibly sought, and the face-to-face relationship is fought for.

The scene in *Ghost Dance* where Derrida delivers his "ghost science" over images of revolutionaries ends on the issue of the body's inability to appropriate the crypt in mourning:

> There is what Abraham and Torok call "incorporation." That is to say, the dead are taken into us but don't become part of us. They just occupy a particular place in our bodies. They can speak for themselves. They can haunt our body and ventriloquise our speech. So the ghost is enclosed in a crypt, which is our body. We become a sort of graveyard for ghosts. A ghost can be not only our unconscious, but more precisely, someone else's unconscious. The other's unconscious speaks in our place. It is not our unconscious, it is the unconscious of the other which plays tricks on us. It can be terrifying. But that's when things start to happen.

Years later, in 2002, at l'Institut national de l'audiovisuel, where he was describing his experience making the Fathy film, Derrida argued the voice was the part of him that most defied re-appropriation:

> Voice raises the violence of exappropriation more than the rest ... Answering for the content of what one says is not the same as recognizing one's voice ... The voice is in effect what is most intimate, most private ... I don't recognize myself in it. (*Penser* 127)[10]

Like the unconscious, exappropriation forces us to mourn something other within us. Our most intimate and private voice always already escapes us.

Nearly twenty years after *Ghost Dance*, in 2002s *Derrida*, the philosopher improvises some remarks on the Echo and Narcissus myth that connect with this explanation of impossible mourning. In the myth, Echo repeats the language of Narcissus, and thus forms her identity based on his words. But like all mourning, there is not a successful incorporation of the other. All appropriation is really an exappropriation, as Echo doesn't simply repeat words, for Derrrida, but borrows his body parts—voice and tone for a new purpose. The body and the senses are intricately bound to the acts of mourning, elsewhere described by Derrida as "eating well." Echo clearly takes body parts from Narcissus only to repeat them but never fully assimilating them—mourning as love. DeArmitt describes it thus,

> It almost seems that Echo "knew" that by reiterating Narcissus's phrases, by allowing his words and sounds to pass through her mouth, she would be able to draw him nearer to her, begin to identify with him, and ultimately respond to her beloved by appropriating his locutions for herself. (128)

The body—gaze, visage, voice, hands—is the medium by which mid-mourning (and love) may occur.

For Derrida, there is no simple appropriation. Appropriation always fails to some small degree: whenever it is identified or recognized it is always done so as appropriation, something that doesn't fit exclusively within that given context. No incorporation—a small failure, as if the cut is more apparent than it should be in order to work as smooth communication. There is no plenitude of meaning within an originary context. Iterability makes any context affected by absence. Thus all communication becomes a form of appropriation without success—exappropriation. Communication is always creating new contexts and thus no ultimate authority over meaning. A cited or repeated communication is never truer in any *one* context. Derrida perhaps first expresses what he means by exappropriation when he defines writing as that which is cut off from its

> 'original' desire-to-say-what-one-means [*vouloir-dire*] and from its participation in a saturable and constraining context. Every sign, linguistic or nonlinguistic, spoken or written (in the current sense of this opposition), in a small or large unit, can be *cited*, put between quotation marks; in so doing in can break with every given context, engendering an infinity of new contexts in a manner which is absolutely illimitable.

This does not imply that the mark is valid outside of a context, but on the contrary that there are only contexts without any center or absolute anchoring [*ancrage*]. (*Limited* 12)

The cut or trace structure of communication is always already conditioned by its failure to fully present its meaning.

Writing became more abstract as it developed, giving the context of its enunciation a performative appeal and authority:

> The same content, formerly communicated by gestures and sounds, will henceforth be transmitted by writing, by successively different modes of notation, from pictographic writing to alphabetic writing, collaterally by the hieroglyphic writing of the Egyptians and the ideographic writing of the Chinese. (*Limited* 4)

In cinema, we assume there is presence because there is more to observe than abstracted writing, because there is voice, tone, pitch, gestures, body language, in short. Now Derrida's body language is becoming iterable, that is, opened up for its meanings. If we are to stay out of presence and examine absence we must ponder what's left out of the cinematic works. Cinema is a form of presence because it contains more traces than what writing can only ever dream to achieve. It pretends to offer more meaning behind the words. It's still a form of absence however because it can only give us images of body parts that are no longer with us, that are dead-like, and thus escape our time. Cinema's body language replaces words as a form of presence because of the illusion of offering an originary context for things. It's spectral because it offers us a glimmer of presence through body parts.

The exappropriable comes about from circumcision as the body parts that cannot and must not return to the self as self. This should give the celebrity pause as they draw a wage from their image. What is really at the heart of spectral cinema, as it concerns Derrida the person and the philosopher, is the exappropriability of (bodily) self-presence. *Not only is the body part processed, tied, copied, spectralized through cinema and image, not only does body language become iterable, not only does the body come back to the self as other, not only is the body no longer of the self, not only is the body touching itself as other, not only is the spectral glance or call an instance of the failure of autobiography, but the body part through cinema cannot be exploited by the self, cannot be understood by the self as self, or as a condition of presence.* Only the other will receive those body parts—gaze, sound, touch, etc. Not only is spectral cinema a giving away of the body—"There should be a film every year," (Dick and Ziering Kofman 112) Derrida himself said—but an exappropriation suggesting a Marxist notion. In *Specters of Marx*, he lays out a working definition of deconstruction:

> [N]amely the deconstruction of the metaphysics of the 'proper,' of logocentrism, linguisticism, phonologism, the demystification or the desedimentation of the autonomic

> hegemony of language (a deconstruction in the course of which is elaborated another concept of the text or the trace, of their originary technization, of iterability, of the prosthetic supplement, but also of the proper and of what was given the name exappropriation). Such a deconstruction would have been impossible and unthinkable in a pre-Marxist space. (*Specters* 115)

This idea of deconstruction as exappropriation resurfaces specifically in his communication on film. Derrida stresses, "That which is absolutely singular about each of us, that which is absolutely idiomatic, the signature for example, is paradoxically that which I cannot reappropriate" (*Penser* 94).[11] Your body cannot be your own endless resource. The body becomes spectral. You cannot tap into a resource that is unstable. It is on the question of cinematic exappropriation in particular that allows Derrida to rearticulate the trace's relation to the decentring of the self. This is tangentially related to stardom, in the star's face, gaze, voice, as productive commodity. This is why minute differences in celebrity and star persona are so common: you can never repeat the same thing without ghostly exploitation. There is something to be said of the exappropriability of the self as a challenge to servitude. Later in *Specters*, he adds,

> [Mourning] is work itself, work in general, the trait by means of which one ought perhaps to reconsider the very concept of production—in what links it to trauma, to mourning, to the idealizing iterability of exappropriation, thus to the spectral spiritualization that is at work in any *tekhne*. (121)

In the Dick and Ziering film, the work of making the film is foregrounded. The filmmakers' engagement with deconstruction is paired with Derrida's own cinematic exploration of deconstructive themes. Patricia Aufderheide situates the film as a challenge to the biography genre: "[*Derrida*] cleverly enacts the difference between experience and documentary, and reveals the power of the storyteller to assert reality … Derrida … repeatedly refuses to cooperate with the filmmakers, revealing instead their presence" (96). In *D'ailleurs, Derrida*, Derrida's acting might be termed "presentational," a kind of documentary performativity that relies on posing and minimal or "accidental" looking at the camera (Waugh 76). But Derrida's performance in *Derrida* could be called confrontational, or representational.

Throughout the film, Derrida not only challenges the notion of biography but of cinematic authorship itself, denying all mastery of the film's meaning. Especially in the Kirby Dick and Amy Ziering film *Derrida*, the work of making the film is foregrounded, such as the scenes where Derrida emphasizes the filmmakers' presence or when he is asked to watch earlier footage of himself. In both of Derrida's biographical documentaries indeterminacy is stressed, as they perpetually defer a complete reading of "Jacques Derrida." Ziering draws on key texts by Derrida (e.g.

Jacques Derrida and *Archive Fever*) and postmodernist cinema, including *Sans soleil* (dir. Marker, France, 1983) and *The Limey* (dir. Soderbergh, US, 1999), to make her documentary.

one can find one's childhood in the look of the eyes.

Moments of obvious exappropriation abound in 2002s *Derrida*, like all the *mise-en-abîme* scenes where Derrida watches himself on the television. After watching a previously recorded scene, he admits to forgetting the time he was asked how he met Marguerite. He says jubilantly, "I like that scene precisely because we don't say anything." Ziering Kofman asks him to improvise some ideas on the subject of body parts. While improvising on the topic of sight relatively early in the film, he says, "It's the Other who knows what our hands and eyes are like …[I]t's very difficult to have an image of our own act of looking or to have a true image of our own hands as they are moving." He stares at the camera as it focuses in on his hands. The irony of this is that the viewers, will know more than him about his eyes and hands, and that this fact stays true especially as the conversation is captured on film. As Nicholas Royle observes in "Blind Cinema,"

> There are numerous moments in the film where we are made especially aware of Derrida's hands, on the move, crucially involved in what he is saying …[W]e are left with a curiously disorienting sense of surface and superficiality, as if with a film over our eyes, the world of Derrida's filmed body, his eyes, hands, mouth and voice. It is as if there were a film over the film, a film over film, a peculiar caul or light cloud, something at once newly visible and newly blinding. (Dick and Ziering Kofman 17–18, 19)

Could that something be cinécircumcision? Royle concludes his essay:

> [T]his image that clings, so long, image of a film in and on film. And, in peculiarly poignant irony, he is of course touching it, fingering the film. Then he turns on the

radio. Biodegradable or not, film is something, as he has telegrammatically noted else-where, 'to be processed.' (Dick and Ziering Kofman 21)

Archive fever can be defined as retracing the other's steps, searching for an "impression that is almost no longer an archive but almost confuses itself with the pressure of the footstep that leaves its still-living mark on a substrate, a sur-face, a place of origin" (Derrida, *Archive* 97). Later, Derrida adds, "The trace no longer distinguishes itself form its substrate" (*Archive* 99). The fleshy part is still there. The heat of the body remains. One recalls here the part in Dick and Ziering Kofman's *Derrida* (or was it Kristen Johnson's documentary collage *Cameraperson* from 2016?) when the philosopher is crossing the street in New York with some friends and colleagues and the cameraperson almost stumbles and falls trying not to get him out of frame. "She sees everything around me but she is totally blind. That's the image of the philosopher who falls in the…(how do you say?) well,—while looking at the star," he says pointing to himself, laughing. While following the star this intently, there is a risk of tripping or falling. Following his footsteps here would be slightly inaccurate—what the makers of *Derrida* decided to follow was his face. The photographic trace of Derrida's face is the philosopher's ultimate circumcision.

Derrida at times wields his body around like it is an authoritative presence that can successfully destabilize the filmmaker's grasp or attempt to inspect *him*: rather, he wants to inspect *them*. He does this by talking, looking critically at the directors, like when he's describing deconstruction for the first time and basically brings the interview to a halt or when he's asked what philosopher his mother would be. He does it by gesturing his arms and claiming he doesn't look like that when he's home alone. His presence is felt when he says, "You mustn't ask me this question, Amy." Derrida: "This is the presupposition and foundation of the law: one is not first identified by one's feet but by the gaze and the mouth, by what addresses the other: directly in the face" (*Copy* 27).

How are all films archival? Naas reminds us the spectral dimension of all archives:

[T]he archive is founded upon a promise—Derrida could have said a faith, an elemen-tary or elemental faith—that precedes and must be thought before all knowledge … [W]hat distinguishes the archive from the trace in general is a certain relationship to power and, especially, political power. (*End of the World* 128, 129)

The digital and new media technologies are changing the nature of the archival thought and the archive is on Derrida's mind more and more near the end, as Naas demonstrates. He shows that thinking about the archive was a foundational act for the philosopher:

> Derrida's entire thinking of the trace in *Of Grammatology* or "Freud and the Scene of Writing" was a rethinking of the archive, or at least of the possibility of the archive, a rethinking of the temporality and spatiality, the iterability and futurity, of what remains. (Naas, *End of the World* 126)

The archive is a constant preoccupation. Derrida gave a major talk on the archive "Trace and Archive" at the Institut National de l'Audiovisuel (INA) on 25 June 2002 in which he speaks at length about his role in Fathy's film.

Derrida describes the logic behind all biographical archiving: "[T]he structure of the archive is spectral" (*Archive* 84). Yerushalmi's biography of Freud links patriarchal origins to Freud's life and work, which effectively turns psychoanalysis into a Jewish science. The archive has spectral inheritance that structures and determines it but without doing so overtly. An important late work in Derrida's oeuvre, the book also features prominently throughout *Derrida*. In fact, out of all the texts quoted by Ziering in the film, *Archive Fever* is used most often. Derrida was obsessive in his effort to archive the documents that came his way. He saved his work on multiple hard drives, fearing that his writing would be irrevocably lost. He even became highly emotional when it was time to give his things over to the archive. This detail is alluded to when the archivist Eddie Yeghiayan mentions how Marguerite related to him that Derrida was having a hard time letting go. Archive fever is an endless search for the other's origin:

> It is the condition for the uniqueness of the printer-printed, of the impression and the imprint, of the pressure and its trace in the unique *instant* where they are not yet distinguished the one from the other, forming in an *instant* a single body of Gradiva's step, of her gait, of her pace (*Gangart*), and of the ground which carries them. The trace no longer distinguishes itself form its substrate. (*Archive* 99)

Fathy's film retraces Derrida's footsteps quite literally. The out of place tile in the house in Algeria haunts Derrida, a spectre of his life and part of the film. The tile out of joint becomes a general element of the film through repetition. The detail goes toward producing an archive effect:

> A single maladjusted tile, out of joint, displaced or badly placed. Who is it? Therefore a return of the law (if this disjointed floor tile was, out of joint, said Hamlet, "I was born to set it right," it was up to me to fix it, I was born to do this. (Derrida and Fathy 90, 91)[12]

Derrida points out in *Tourner les mots* that the tile doesn't constitute an event because it never really had an origin itself. Rather, it can be thought of as kind of bodily motion or memory without genesis. He even connects it with everything out of joint, *tout qui va mal*, in his life:

Him alone—he specifies that his brother and his sister have no memories of this floor tile, that they never noticed it—he was its singular recipient, he noticed it, from that moment on he was called forth, elected and vowed to forever adjust this maladjustment of justice, an idea if not an image invariably connected to the law and justice. (Michaud 82)[13]

To what extent does this shot, this *punctum* morphing into *studium*, haunt the film? Spectral cinema must be haunted by something like a *punctum*, something that addresses you in a singular way.

Both *D'ailleurs, Derrida* and *Derrida* include scenes of Derrida in his library, presenting it:

[*D'ailleurs, Derrida*] shows Derrida in his attic study that is awash in books, and in a garden shed where he keeps manuscripts, correspondence, students' theses, etc. "I never throw anything away," he says, and muses on his desire for things that don't need him, that can live without and after him. For him an archive registers a relation to the impossible: his death. (Lilly 394)

Another way the archive can be conceived is by what the film leaves out, but that haunts it. Fathy explains how even the cut footage engages with the film archive:

An exchange, therefore, between the visible and the invisible, appearance of the disappearance. In a conversation, Derrida was saying, a descendant of death, the image is always a shroud, that which reveals as it veils, that which hides the face and exhibits it at once. The veil printed from the traces of the face that is caught. The image regards us and reveals the other within us. Who hasn't been surprised by one's own photo? Each image takes an unknown part of the self and fixes it, a strange part that doesn't allow itself to be reappropriated, because it already belongs to another world, the world of the icon and simulacra. This conversation facing the ocean bristling with dolphins was equally cut from the film. The images that remain speak for the ones that were cut, they contain within them the deleted ones like within mourning. The survivor keeps within herself the dead, carries them and guards them. How many dead are we made from? (Derrida and Fathy 164)[14]

Already during the production, the spectral guides the process of archiving.

In 2005, Safaa Fathy made a one-hour film *De tout cœur* that comprised three filmed interviews with Derrida. In the first interview, from 2002, Derrida spoke about the Israeli-Palestine conflict, appealing to those who wanted to see all violence cease in the area. The second interview, from a 2001 conference, shows Derrida answering a question from a fellow academic on the topic of cloning. He proceeds to deconstruct the discourse around cloning that claims that clones, unlike "natural" human beings, will be too similar and their behaviour will be repetitive. In the final segment, filmed in Paris in 2000, Derrida and Jean-Luc Nancy answer questions from an audience on the theme of hospitality and the body. He claims that love is akin to a heart transplant. The expression *tu es mon coeur* reveals the ways in which the heart belongs to the other. In each part, Derrida meditates on the meaning of the heart and the word *coeur*.

In fact, a few films have been made since Derrida's death in 2004 that either use his name (*Film Socialisme*) or actual footage of him from different sources (*Love in the Post: From Plato to Derrida* [dir. Callaghan, 2014]). These works, in a sense, get the ghost going, reminding us, through Derrida's voice and image, body parts, that the body of work is unfinished and continues even now and no doubt in the future. These films have sought to make new connections between the philosophical text and film. *De tout coeur* is particularly interesting because it aims to bring forward the body, or at least a body part into this discourse of the growing or undead *body* of work.

The choices of what happens to our dead body (cremation, burial) and indeed choices surrounding how we die now make our relation to death more complex and richer than ever. But this relation to our own death and our dead body remains at the level of the imaginative, for the loss of control following our death means we are always someone else's responsibility. Michael Naas spells out Derrida's relation to his dead body:

> The other is the one who will survive me, and I can only then *imagine* what this other will do with my remains, since the moment I begin to predict or envision any future or propose any hypothesis as to how the other will respond, I already begin to take the place of the other and so am already in the realm of the phantasm. (*End of the World* 69)

Even (or especially) in death, Derrida's body (and his cinematic corpus) is in the hands of the other.

Laurence Simmons suggests the face is the most important figure or trope in Derrida's thinking of the body. It is after all Levinas' most influential concept on Derrida's writings: "Levinas' face is not simply the biological or natural face, nor is it a *prosopon*, it is the emblem of the appearance of the idea of infinity that exists within the subject, that fundamentally resists comprehension" (133). Simmons stresses the ways Derrida's conception of the face is based on absolute alterity and therefore a form of ethical violence:

> As an irrecuperable intrusion in our world, which lies beyond our full comprehension, but whose otherness we are responsible for preserving, Derrida's rehabilitation of the ghost becomes an ethical injunction in that it occupies the place of the Levinasian Other. (134)

The face is the site of an intense spectral dissymmetry. The face as ghost, dismembered, body part, site of thought, finds its most fitting haunt in cinema.

In Hollywood film, the male gaze has historically structured the way the viewer sees the story world. Whether it be the prized possession that all the characters are fighting for or the female love interest, nearly all narrative events are seen through the focalizer of the male gaze. Feminist film theorist Laura Mulvey has analyzed the phenomenon of the male gaze in Hollywood film in her influential essay "Visual Pleasure and Narrative Cinema" (1975). The gaze into the camera is a self-reflexive return to the gaze of the observer, the filmmaker, and the viewer. Drawing on the essay, Mulvey might argue that such a postmodern gesture is meant to let the viewer know that he, too, is exposed, no longer voyeuristically hidden in the dark. It asks us to ask ourselves something about the interior life of the subject as more than fetish object.

The girl in the Bissau market in *Sans soleil* is so enigmatic because of the spectral structure that makes meaning enigmatic in the first place. Some films are self-consciously archival. *Sans soleil* shows how the gaze can inaugurate a narrative. The filmmaker wrongly believes that he can observe and study the ladies in the market without them studying him in return. The narrator asks,

> How to film the ladies of Bissau? Apparently, the magical function of the eye was working against me there. It was in the market places of Bissau and Cape Verdi that I could stare at them again with equality. I see her. She saw me. She knows that I see her. She drops me her glance, but just at an angle where it is still possible to act as though it was not addressed to me. And at the end: the real glance, straightforward, that lasted a twenty-fourth of a second, the length of a film frame ... Frankly, have you ever heard of anything stupider than to say to people as they teach in film schools, not to look at the camera?

Her look lasts just a single frame, the narrator claims, but that second points out the women's indestructability.

In *Grizzly Man*, Treadwell's footage contrasts Herzog's. For all the attempts at explaining Treadwell's psyche and motivations, for all the counter argumentation that Herzog puts forth, Treadwell's footage still has a spectral power more enthralling than Herzog's. The archive effect revives Treadwell and his gaze becomes more powerful. That is why I would not say *Grizzly Man* is a Herzog film. The ghost of Treadwell is too strong to be silenced. There is no need to give the ultimate, final authority of the film to Herzog. Could the auteur-actor division be under erasure in this instance? Derrida describes the right of inspection of *D'ailleurs, Derrida*, but this type of spectrality could easily apply to *Grizzly Man*:

> Once the film is out there, you see, the film also sees. Beyond the mirroring effects and the *mise-en-abîme*, there is that incredible dissymmetry, an inversion of the typical 'points of view' that many judge to be intolerable. This seems arrogant, despite the obvious modesty and sincerity of the protagonists. The film is the subject and the one

with the eyes that observe us, that reappear, eyes that see rather than are seen or are visible. We are seen by the film. It regards me, concerns, and judges me, from the eyes of the Author, of the virtual Spectator, of the Actor, especially the Actor. (Derrida and Fathy 125)[15]

The actor certainly has a power stronger than the *Auteur* or indeed any other element of the film that creates the Law of inspection.

Jeong and Andrew point out that Herzog himself admits a certain defeat (as the film's director) in light of Treadwell's remarkable footage:

When mysterious black spots on Treadwell's tent are revealed to be the traces of a pet fox's paws, Herzog rightly admires the secret beauty of this 'seemingly empty' but 'glorious improvised moment' that no studio reconstruction could ever foresee. 'For a filmmaker, things fall into your lap that you could never dream of. There is something like an inexplicable magic of cinema … Sometimes images themselves develop their own life, their own mysterious start.' (12)

Moreover, language, speech in this case, keeps Treadwell from becoming-animal (5) but Treadwell's footage evinces a contradictory becoming-animal. In the footage, we see Treadwell frolic with foxes, adapt to nature, encounter death, and bury his hands in bear excrement. Jeong and Andrew write, Becoming-animal means abandoning identity and individuation (7), but I would add, in cinema, it's the gaze of the other that ensures this. "Treadwell would stand outside every enclosure, a schizophrenic nomad, a grizzly man not to be penned in by any institution or on any reservation, no matter how vast," (8) Jeong and Andrew observe. The video works as a promise, a commencement. Herzog, who dismisses almost everything Treadwell says, ironically assists Treadwell's resurrection. "Overwhelming indifference which Herzog sees in the bear's blank stare may signal something more than the absolute antipode of civilization," (11) stress Jeong and Andrew.

The same kind of unexpected looks (Treadwell looking at viewers that are absent yet none the less present, viewers looking at absent-present Treadwell, virtual viewers looking at Treadwell, virtual viewers looking at us) find a corollary in *Memoirs of the Blind*, where Derrida describes the blinding quality of drawing and the autoportrait. When the artist is confronted with the other looking back at him, like in Treadwell's video, there is a communication with the self as other, as ghost, and, in this instance, as animal, too.

In *Grizzly Man*, much of what we see is Treadwell entering frame, posing for the camera. The act of posing is uncommonly foregrounded. Some scenes show Treadwell posing, just posing, as if what matters is the posing. Treadwell's promise also overrides Herzog's. In *Right of Inspection*, Derrida suggests posing is a precondition for a law of reading.[16] The *Acteur* becomes a presence and has the power of an archive. Suspense is so powerful because it allows for indeterminacy, the unfinished, hope. He calls it an epochal suspense. The teletechnological inaugurates an era of faith specifically where we no longer thought belief dwelled. The documentary genre has in fact been marked by deconstructive belief, as per Baron.

The archive is always virtual, always a retracing of steps. A matter of private exposure, the gaze into the lens seems to start an archival effect. That is, the beginning, commencement, commandment of the archive derives from the virtual contact, a desire to expose and slice. But as Derrida reminds us, it's only a spectral effect; being looked at by someone who is not there. There is no face-to-face even for the characters of a film, as Derrida shows in *Right of Inspection* (28). But the subject looking into the lens begins a spectral communication, as Lippit and Saghafi both show. The origin of the archive, the film's narrative focus, the film's arguments and logic, the world of the film relies on believing the gaze has something to do with *me*, at the moment of reception. That gaze rests upon a delicate operation. Just enough is taken away to still have the semblance of completeness and absence of mutilation.

Like the signature, the image inhabits a borderline between life and work. On the post-structuralist autobiography, Linda Anderson observes,

> While the autobiographical subject (as in Rousseau's Confessions, for instance) is always engaged in going beyond itself into other discourses, or into discourse as a form of otherness, philosophical discourse is seen by Derrida as dependent on moments which defy its own systematic coherence, a specificity, or autobiographical trace, which remains despite the assumption of universality, and which it can never decisively overcome. (80)

The life and work division assumed by traditional philosophy and science is blurred from the moment the subject is named: "The 'I' is always a place of self-division for Derrida, an addressor *and* an addressee, a name which, after it is spoken, also requires to be heard" (82). The name and the image of "Jacques Derrida" lives on in the other.

Jean-Paul Fargier's film version of *Memoirs of the Blind* shows Derrida sitting in a television studio reading from a teleprompter extracts and summarized arguments from his essay "Mémoires d'aveugle: L'autoprotrait et autres ruines." Words are included, but then again why sit and lecture at the camera—a most uncinematic style if there ever was one? Yet, what is added through cinema? Body language: eyes and hands, mostly. These body parts are depicted in a most curious fashion. These are the contextual elements that typically get lost in writing. Superadded, eyes and hands don't complete the context, don't fill in what is typically missing, however. Who was Derrida addressing? What was cut from his discourse? The gestures and gazes are also supplementary, that is, communicated, written, iterable.

There is blindness in the autoportrait. Not only because he can't see the viewers, but because the camera cuts, frames, parcels him up into parts, a glance is extracted, a hand movement excised, a skin is removed. We look at his whitening hair, his head and nose, his hands, of course, even shoulders and ears. He can't see himself, the proper self—he will never know what we saw of him. As his full self is cut up and parcelled out, disseminated, his eyes and hands connect the film and the essay. They are the links, or joints. Derrida mimics the scene of painting as a new context for painting is presented to us. The paintings of Jesus healing the blind depict the icon applying or holding his hand over the blind's eyes. Derrida holds out his hands. The hands aid in regaining sight. Elsewhere, he examines the fixed eye of the subject/painter in the autoportraits of Henri Fantin-Latour. In fixing his gaze of himself, the painter sees nothing, nothing other than what he wants to see. At this point the camera frames only half of Derrida's face, the blind subject before the lens. *We see nothing other than a gaze that looks at us.* These are eyes and hands that see but that cannot see themselves. The hands in the painting see in their own blind ways. These are traces by the blind and in a certain way for the blind, too.

In *On Touching—Jean-Luc Nancy*, Derrida explains there is a respect in tact. What is the touch without touch, as in a caress (66–69)? Real touching blemishes, imposes, probes, violates, while the touch without touch maintains a respectful distance toward the other. In logocentric thought, vision and touch are opposed— Derrida has always been interested in examining the sensible and non-sensible: he wanted to articulate a touching sight whenever possible. Lippit notes that it is the same eyeline gaze between Derrida and Pascale Ogier that creates an immediate intense connection that defies space and time. In "Spectrographies," Derrida recounts this very personal experience of filming the scene with Ogier, and then encountering her ghost, again, years later and after her death. Derrida writes lucidly, "[M]y freedom springs from the condition of this responsibility which is born of heteronomy in the eyes of the other, in the other's sight. This gaze is spectrality itself" (Derrida and Stiegler 122). In *Cinema without Reflection*, Lippit sees in the eyeline the possibility of bodily presence:

> This prosthesis of the eye, or spectacle, allows for the encounter between two bodies, an exchange of looks, an eye for an eye. Like photographic light, and the light of stars, the eye-line ensures the survival of a look, even when the subjects of the look may have long disappeared. Plus surplus light. (10)

In cinema especially, there is a touching aspect to the gaze—the eyeline technique secures spectral connection. This goes back to the touch without penetration or mutilation. A haptic experience that nevertheless maintains a distance: like circumcision, this touch will not go as far as use, deface, exploit, mutilate the other. Circumcision is understood as a kind of self-touching because the moment cannot be recalled easily or at all—we generally recall it to ourselves. Circumcision self-touches and it is also violence toward the self because it gives itself to the other, as in the Levinasian face-to-face encounter. But as a viewer of Derrida, can we not then say that we are responsible for a certain part of him, here alluding to all the metaphors of pregnancy and contagion that that might entail?

When Derrida is asked a question about what kind of film he would like to see about philosophers, Derrida says a film wherein they talk about their sex lives. Ziering Kofman asks him if he would like to talk about his sex life. Derrida covers his mouth and returns to silence. A scene later in the film illustrates presence and a counter-signing logical beautifully. Kirby Dick asks Derrida, "If you had a choice what philosopher would you have liked to been your mother?" Derrida takes a very long time to answer, initially scoffing at the question, then laughing, and then thinking deeply, until he says, "It's a very good question in fact." Not until he's asked something which he approves of does he answer, not until in some ways does he repeat the question himself, not until his presence is in some way irrefutable, does he answer. By antagonistically refusing to answer questions, or by not answering them in a certain, "American fashion," suggests there is always more that is left out, something present (the body?) yet unknown, which prevents closure.

But how will this affect the archive? Some subjects, indeed, only exist in the film archive, and thus, make us contemplate the importance of the vast archive of sounds and images in the two official Derrida archives, one at Irvine and the other at IMEC. All new discoveries will be spectral in a sense, but perhaps the sound and image recordings will be spectral in stronger ways, which in itself will guide the kinds of extensions of the body. This is a common thing when it comes to film stars, but almost entirely uncommon in philosophy. Could something as paradoxical or miraculous as spectrality dictate the future direction of Derrida's corpus.

Derrida uses intentional disparity to create an "archive effect" based around Derrida's biography and personal life. While the filmmakers seek to draw out his true personality in the interviews that emphasize closeness, then by replaying portions of the film, the film also creates multiple levels of disparity, both intentional and temporal. We can never know for sure what Derrida has seen and how he has guided the editorial process. This strategy of showing Derrida being shown the scenes creates a disparity as all the footage becomes potentially "old" and "new" at once. Ziering asks him about origin of deconstruction very early on in the film. Derrida tells her he needs to make certain remarks about the artificial nature of the situation before he can answer her question. Instead of a concise explanation of deconstruction, we get a long dissolve with different footage of Derrida preparing to give a lecture in his classroom. The dissolve would normally be used as a quick transition, lasting three to four seconds, but here the length points to the apparatus, the technical aspect of editing, indicating the underlying structure of the film, and thus complicating our notions of linearity.

After a very breezy, fast-paced start that positions itself as a traditional *cinéma vérité* biography, the film takes an uncommon turn into reversals, slow motion interludes, long improvisations, technical problems, and *mise-en-abîme* sections. "New" footage is at once what seems to be presently unfolding and what could have happened long ago but that nonetheless guides the whole process, as if every moment is potentially ripe with new meanings, discoveries, surprises, and shocks. The last shot of the film, where he is asked about the trauma of his life, was likely filmed very early in the production, for instance. We never get the sense that we are progressing toward a final destination that reveals the "real" Derrida in an effective *cinéma vérité* mode. And like many documentaries and films in general, the significant amount of deleted footage can still be felt in the "saved" footage. Disparity exists between the interviews and the film's overall structure, and within the interviews themselves, through Derrida's performance.

Simply put, Ziering's questions could be too conventional for him. In a deleted scene, Ziering asks Derrida, "When we spoke in Paris and you did that improv in the apartment, you said something off-hand, you said, 'It's very American of you Amy to just give me a topic and ask me to speak.'... Why would it be very American?" Derrida seems to have his answer ready:

> What I mean by American—maybe my use of the word was a bit abusive—what I called 'American' here were two things, one which could be considered abusive, the other less so. The abusive use was about the utilitarian, manipulative attitude. 'Okay, I need this—do it!' 'Here's a term, go ahead. Action!' Everybody who makes a film does this. But cinema is American. It's more American than other things. Today, the world's experience of cinema is largely, as you well know, whether one likes it or not, shaped by American culture. So that would be the, how do you say, abusive aspect of my vague usage of the term 'American.' But the less vague and less abusive use of the term has to do with something I noticed in American universities even in 1956, the first year I was there. I noticed in academic or social situations, that someone would ask someone else, a professor to a student, a student to a professor, or a student to a student—'Could you elaborate on these things?' 'Here's a word and go and work' from the mention of just one word: 'please elaborate.' Even now, during my office hours, Americans will just come, 'Could you tell me more about this or that? Could you elaborate?' This doesn't happen in France. You don't just say, 'Could you elaborate?' I don't even know how to say it in French. I'm not saying it never happens, but it's much less frequent in France. It happens sometimes, and this is 'American' in the first abusive sense, but it happens in radio or televised interviews, with hurried, manipulative journalists who think that because someone is a philosopher, you can ask them to suddenly speak about Being. As if you can push a button and there's a readymade discourse on being or love. No. I have nothing readymade. So, on the one hand there's the abusive use of the term

'American' that refers to all of the cinematic, journalistic, manipulative attitudes. And a more strict sense of the term 'American' which refers to what happens in the university, when someone just asks someone to elaborate on something. Voila.

He is asked to elaborate based on one word. It instantly makes the one who asks, the one who specifically isn't developing what could possibly be a very complex idea, the authority. Dick and Ziering count on, depend on his presence even while he shows them that the present is divided. Hence, their different approaches in the interview scenes compared to the editing and montage, the film's structure. In the interviews, they ask their questions like good American documentary journalists, but something has been registered in the process, for the film's structure doesn't reflect this vulture-like tendency. *Who is the author?*

Derrida is shown what seems like avoiding tough or personal questions. At one point, he berates Ziering for asking "such a question." And at the end he refuses to go into the traumas of his life. "Once again, I will not be able to," he says. The fact that there is always a script and direction behind the filmmakers' questions is rarely mentioned. The repetition of the Derrida excerpts accentuates the fact of representation and repetition. We question whether Ziering and Dick are the true authors and whether or not Derrida countersigns as much as they "create." *Derrida* suggests for there to be authorship/authority/ownership, there must also always be a countersigning presence. Derrida did have final cut of the film and the filmmakers even filmed the signing of the contract (although it was later cut) (Dick and Ziering Kofman 24–25). There was an agreement but the contract signing scene was excluded from the film, raising many questions about the true author, signer of *Derrida*.

As Jonathan Lahey Dronsfield points out,

> [T]his does not mean that his signature is nowhere to be seen. Derrida is seen to be refusing to discuss certain things about his life, for instance his relationship with his wife. Derrida is at that moment editing what he will or will not divulge about himself. It is an editorial decision, even if it is not his decision to include [the signing of the contract] scene in the film. But the editing begins before the camera starts rolling. (220)

Derrida and the film's strategy is this: the documentary subject ironically points out the filmmakers' absence in their own film while emphasizing his own presence that will also eventually turn to absence and exappropriation. Tellingly, Ziering cut the quote about representation from *Writing and Difference* as if she were cutting the admission of a script or a set of representational conventions that facilitates the film's unique effect, which is that Derrida simply calls them out or denies biographical coherence, which are both indeed the cases. But it's more complex than that. Derrida deconstructs a whole documentary tradition that claims a certain spontaneity. He countersigns, thus showing how spontaneity is written, authored, signed.[17]

Ziering has stated one of her intentions for the documentary was to narrow-in on critical thinking, celebrate the French intellectualism of Derrida in the face of 21st century US politics embodied best in the Bush II administration. Derrida's interview style is constructed as an exemplary example of the deconstructive or spectral subject. Ziering uses these moments as the strength that propels her film. Spectrality, its structure, its example, emerges as something worth preserving in itself. This is why in *Derrida* the ghost won't be exorcized. The *mise-en-abime* reflexively helps this dimension of the film by suggesting always there is more to discover, more to Derrida, and more than one.

Reviews of *Derrida* seem to agree that deconstruction gets short thrift, but it does convey Derrida's intelligence and charisma. Owen Gleiberman maintains the film offers no understanding of the philosophy or the philosophical-institutional context of deconstruction. He writes,

> There's a lot of obscurity to bask in. Like his analytic godfathers, Foucault and Sartre (who are never even mentioned in the film—yes, it's that slipshod), Derrida has a singular knack for stating an oblique epiphany 12 different ways. Once you've heard him spit out enough phrases like "the one forgets to remember itself to itself," you may start to long for a bit of history about how this man, with his circular wisps of hyper-cogitation, turned the academic world inside out. You won't get it from *Derrida*.

While calling the film "entertaining," David Sterritt cautions, "[T]he things he says on camera aren't nearly as profound as the passages quoted from his books." We should address whether the film fails to explain deconstruction. Does it offer any good definitions? Clear and succinct ones are to be found in the deleted scenes, like when Derrida, sitting on a porch, explains how deconstruction acknowledges the non-being of being and how it radically makes room for alterity. In this clip, this single shot alone, which runs around six minutes, the arch deconstructionist offers what can only be described as a kind of philosophical pitch with TED-talk succinctness.

Why is it that the filmmakers deliberately avoid defining deconstruction? My argument is at this point in time, by the time of the mid-1990s deconstruction, post-structuralism, and post-modernism were no longer one thing. That is, deconstruction had already been applied to the visual arts, to architecture, to law, and had in a sense graduated from being a purely "textual" and linguistic-philosophical tool to one which encompassed, in short, everything, transforming it into a transdisciplinary philosophy. The filmmakers of *Derrida* enter the scene of deconstruction at this point. Rick Groen, writing for *The Globe and Mail*, admits he knows nothing of deconstruction, suggesting his knowledge of it was Woody Allen's *Deconstructing*

Harry (US, 1997) until he saw Dick and Ziering's film. Still, Groen makes a key insight:

> [T]he picture's charm lies in the continuing by-play between the filmmakers and their subject, with each side doing its best to deconstruct the other. Of course, the advantage goes to Derrida, and not just because of his sizeable brain ... Better yet, when the interviewer raises a query and the lens closes in on his dark eyes, you can almost see the cerebral engine at work—pondering, sifting, weighing, rejecting, accepting, and only then answering ... He's always aware and wary of the thing, of this 'archiving machine.' And he's predictably scathing about the cinema's pretense of vérité ...[T]he directors walk a fine line between acknowledging that pretense and maintaining it. So, on one hand, they shoot him before a succession of mirrors, analyzing the myth of Narcissus while his own image is fractured and multiplied. Yet, on the other, they strive to squeeze out a few concrete and personal facts ...

Groen ends his review praising Derrida's interview style and performance and pointing to the film's undeniable uniqueness. Groen describes Derrida's monologue on love thusly: "[A]n eternity on film, and a landmark extension of the sound bite into a sound chomp. In the proud annals of philosophy, that's small step; in the reductive world of the camera, it's a giant leap." For a critic unfamiliar with Derrida's philosophical output, he perfectly sums up one of the ways *Derrida* puts deconstruction into action. Rather than explaining it, rather than offering cutesy definitions or (worse still) cutesy animated sequences illustrating how Derrida is the Zorro to the Western philosophic canon or (even worse) talking head sequences by every Derridean under the sun, *Derrida* is a film that is still using deconstructive techniques, approaches, not to define it, but to explore the world at hand.

Derrida also channels relatively late aspects of deconstruction that emphasize spectrality, apparitions, the other, and the future. The excerpts Ziering reads are from "Circumfession," *Archive Fever*, *The Gift of Death*, etc. What was misunderstood by many critics as a lack of context or failure to spell out Derrida's philosophy was actually the film's attempt to explore these later themes in the philosopher's output, a much more ambitious task arguably than merely summarizing Derrida. Amy Ziering describes the cat and mouse chase of the film:

> Derrida could not help but call attention to and reference the filmmaking process at any and all given opportunities. Pointing a camera at Jacques pretty much was like throwing chum to a shark—he couldn't refrain from in some way calling attention to the technological machinations. As an increasing amount of the footage began to inevitably refer to this fact, Kirby and I ultimately realized that there was in fact no way to avoid actually taking it up or, for that matter, even embracing it as a structural element of the film. In addition, since Jacques playfully sparred with me on camera throughout the film, and since our filmmaker/subject relationship seemed to also

nicely reflect and comment on certain prominent and fundamental themes in Jacques' work (e.g., issues of supplementarity, authorship, translation, signature, parasite/host relations), Kirby and I decided, after careful deliberation, to reference the filmmaker/ subject relationship in our film in both subtle and overt ways. (Dick and Ziering Kofman 32)

Because it is a commentary on the genre's very criteria, because it is its conventions that he countersigns, the film, in a sense, countersigns, in one fell swoop, an entire genre of filmmaking. Could Ziering and Dick have predicted making a film that seemed to be unmaking itself as it went along? In other words, could they have anticipated the arrival of a force, of the future, of the other who would counter-sign? Who is left to counter-sign the film? If an actor can counter-sign who else can? The spectator? Derrida says he doesn't know who will be watching this, properly registering his relation to the other. Jeong and Andrew could be describing Derrida at this moment when they refer to Treadwell:

He as specter and we as ghosts encounter each other in this real-time play of *différance*, in which he came to us too late and we have not yet come to him. This is an encounter in and of a third kind, a time that unfolds in the future perfect tense, for he will already have died before our watching him, the spectre, and we ghosts will already have watched him before his death. Such an impossible encounter in an impossible time is possible only because of the passage through death of a non-conscious quasi-being. So we could conclude: only becoming-specter can bring about absolutely new encounters—with another being, with another time and with another territory— which are outside of, though immanent in, our being, our time and our territory. (10)

By internalizing the ghostly viewer, who will come after the production, he also imagines his own spectral existence, which is the only relation we can possibly have to our own death, and archive.

Here spectrality functions like in *Archive Fever*, as Ziering chases after Jacques Derrida, looking for impressions of who he is. She is haunted by his ghost, a version of Derrida that propels her and her film, perhaps brought on by the filmmaking process itself. Derrida asserts his right as a spectre of *différance*, a spectre to come, a spectre of the future instead of the locatable past. A spectre of the future, always. The lack of an "origin tale" means *Derrida* specifically will continue to haunt us "tomorrow, in times to come, or perhaps never." Derrida, always aware of the deathly aspects of film, said in yet another deleted filmed interview:

I feel watched. Like right now. What am I doing? You're filming me. Even if I live to be very old, which I hope, these images will most likely live longer than I. So there will be people who can see these images when I'm dead. That's inscribed in the structure of what we're doing. Death is here. We are filming someone who we know will die before the archive. (Dick and Ziering Kofman 46)

Notes

1. "Le film est un art de la coupure … de l'interuption qui pourtant laisse vivre … Et on sait très bien que tout revient à l'art du montage, à l'art de l''edition', de l''editing', au sens Anglais."

2. "Au-delà de tout ce que j'ai pu indirectement apprendre, comprendre ou approcher du cinéma, rien ne vaut cette expérience inflexible qui laisse peu de retrait au corps. J'ai pu comprendre beaucoup de choses sur le cinéma en général, sur la technologie, sur le marché … En ce sens, ce fut un 'film d'apprentissage.'"

3. "Et comment filmer les mots qui deviennent des images, qui soient inséparables du corps, non seulement de la personne qui les dit, mais du corps, de l'ensemble iconique, et qui néanmois restent des mots, avec leur sonorité, le ton, le temps des mots?"

4. "Le film me dit: 'Tu ne peux pas te réapproprier cette chose-là. L'idiome, ton idiome absolu, ce que tu es, ce que tu penses, ce que tu dis depuis la première circoncision, tout cela qui est ton idiome, qui est ton propre absolu, eh bien, c'est un propre qui n'apparaît qu'à l'autre et donc qui n'est pas réappropriable, tu ne peux pas te réapproprier ton propre, ton propre appartient à l'autre.'"

5. "[L]e film dit, en français et en anglais, c'est naturellement une part de moi, indéniablement, de cet idiome que je ne peux pas me réapproprier et que le film me montre, me renvoie, mais aussi que ça part de moi … Moi, je peux mourir à chaque instant, la trace reste là. La coupure est là. C'est une part de moi qui est coupée de moi et qui donc part de moi aux deux sens du terme: elle procède, elle émane de moi, mais en même temps en se séparant, en se coupant, en se détachant de moi. Et donc, cette part de moi, je la gagne, je la retrouve narcissiquement, mais je la perds en même temps."

6. "En toutes lettres sur l'écran d'abord en majuscule PAROLE ensuite en minuscule *écriture*; de même: ÂME *corps*, DEDANS *dehors*, MASCULIN *féminin*, PRÉSENCE *absence*, SENSIBLE *intelligible*, etc."

7. "La déconstruction s'amorce en présentant dans un premier temps comme primaire ce que la métaphysique dit être secondaire."

8. "À l'écran nous voyons que les lettres devenues trop instables tombent de leur place et se mélangent."

9. "un discours d'économie et non d'excès."

10. "La violence de l'expropriation relève plus de la voix que du rest … [R]épondre du contenu de ce qu'on dit, ce n'est pas la même chose que reconnaître sa voix … La voix, c'est en effect ce qu'il y a de plus intime, de plus privé …[J]e ne me reconnais pas là-dedans."

11. "Ce qui est absolument singulier chez chacun de nous, ce qui est absolument idiomatique, la signature disons, c'est paradoxalement ce que je ne peux pas me réapproprier."

12. "[U]n seul carreau mal ajusté, disjoint, désajusté, déplacé ou mal placé. Qui est-ce?… Donc un retour du droit (si le carrelage désaccordé, disjoint, désajointé était *out of joint*, eût dit Hamlet, '*I was born to set it right*', c'était à moi de réparer, j'étais né pour ça."

13. "Lui seul—il précise que son frère et sa soeur ne se souviennent pas de ce carreau, qu'ils ne l'ont même jamais remarqué—, il en fut l'unique destinataire, il a été remarqué par lui, désormais appelé, élu, voué par lui à la tâche infinie d'ajuster ce désajustement du juste, idée sinon image immanquablement tangent à celle de la loi et de la justice."

14. "Un échange, donc, entre le visible et l'invisible, l'apparition de la disparition. Dans une conversation, Derrida disait que, telle une descendante de la mort, l'image est toujours un suaire, ce qui révèle en voilant, ce qui cache le visage et l'exhibe à la fois. Le voile imprimé par les traits du

visage qui surprend. L'image nous regarde et révèle l'autre en soi. Qui n'a jamais été surprise par sa propre photo? Chaque image prend une part inconnue de soi et la fixe, une part étrangère qui ne se laisse pas réapproprier, parce qu'elle appartient déjà à un autre monde, le monde de l'icône et du simulacra. Cette conversation face à l'océan hérissé de dauphins a été également coupée du film. Les images qui restent parlent pour celles qui ont disparu, elles contiennent en elles les disparues comme le deuil. Le survivant prend en soi le mort, le porte et le garde. De combien de morts sommes-nous faits?"

15. "[D]ès qu'il y a le film, voyez-vous, le film aussi regarde. Au-delà des effets de miroir et d'abîme, il y a cette incroyable dissymétrie, une inversion des 'points de vue' que beaucoup jugeront intolérable. Arrogante même, malgré la modestie évidente et sincère des protagonistes. Le film, c'est lui le sujet, à lui sont les yeux qui vous observent, ils lui reviennent, des yeux voyants plus tôt que vus ou visibles. Nous sommes vus par lui, nous sommes vus du film. Il me regarde d'abord, il me concerne et il me juge. Par les yeux de l'Auteur, du Spectateur virtuel, de l'Acteur même, de l'Acteur surtout."

16. Derrida explores the expression *mise en demeure* in *Right of Inspection*: "[The photographic machine] is a machine for making talk—inexhaustibly. And what interests me about the words *mise en demeure* is the *mise* or 'positioning,' otherwise called the *pose*, all the poses, including the photographic one, it reinscribes them all, both the positioning of bodies and whatever else is placed—the bets, the sequence of moves, the risks taken, the game that is calculated on the surface of a checkerboard, the escalating stakes, the outbidding, the challenge, and the 'patience' (the game but also the successful outcome) of a bout with chance. Yes, the pose, position, supposition, the place of each *subject* ..." (Derrida and Plissart 3).

17. For a discussion of realism and the supposed lack of style in Artaud's theatre, see "The Theater of Cruelty and the Closure of Representation" in *Writing and Difference*.

Bibliography

Anderson, Linda. *Autobiography*. London and New York: Routledge, 2001.

Aufderheide, Patricia. *Documentary Film: A Very Short Introduction*. Oxford and New York: Oxford University Press, 2007.

Baron, Jaimie. "Contemporary Documentary Film and 'Archive Fever': History, the Fragment, the Joke." *The Velvet Light Trap* 60 (Fall 2007): 13–24.

———. *Archive Effect: Found Footage and the Audiovisual Experience of History*. London and New York: Routledge, 2014.

Baum, Devorah. "Circumcision Anxiety." *Textual Practice* 27.4 (2013): 695–713.

Bennington, Geoffrey, and Jacques Derrida. *Jacques Derrida*. Trans. Geoffrey Bennington. Chicago, IL: University of Chicago Press, 1993.

Burt, Jonathan. "Morbidity and Vitalism: Derrida, Bergson, Deleuze, and Animal Film Imagery." *Configurations* 14.1–2 (Winter-Spring 2006): 157–179.

Callaghan, Joanna, dir. *Love in the Post*. 2014. DVD. Heraclitus Pictures, 2014.

DeArmitt, Pleshette. *The Right to Narcissism: A Case for an Im-possible Self-Love*. New York: Fordham University Press, 2014.

Derrida, Jacques. *Writing and Difference.* Trans. Alan Bass. London: Routledge, 1978.

———. *Limited Inc.* Evanston, IL: Northwestern University Press, 1988.

———. *Archive Fever: A Freudian Impression.* Trans. Eric Prenowitz. Chicago, IL: University of Chicago Press, 1996.

———. *On Touching—Jean-Luc Nancy.* Trans. Christine Irizarry. Stanford, CA: Stanford University Press, 2005.

———. *Specters of Marx: The State of the Debt, the Work of Mourning, and the New International.* Trans. Peggy Kamuf. New York and London: Routledge, 2006.

———. *Copy, Archive, Signature: A Conversation on Photography.* Trans. Jeff Fort. Stanford, CA: Stanford University Press, 2010.

———. *Penser à ne pas voir: Écrits sur les arts du visible 1979–2004.* Paris: Éditions de la différence, 2013.

Derrida, Jacques, and Bernard Stiegler. *Echographies of Television.* Trans. Jennifer Bajorek. Cambridge: Polity Press, 2002.

Derrida, Jacques, and Marie-François Plissart. *Right of Inspection.* Trans. David Wills. New York: Monacelli Press, 1998.

Derrida, Jacques, and Safaa Fathy. *Tourner les mots: au bord d'un film.* Paris: Éditions Galilée, 2000.

Dick, Kirby, and Amy Ziering Kofman, dirs. *Derrida.* 2002. DVD. Zeitgeist Video, 2003.

———, eds. *Derrida: Screenplay and Essays on the Film Derrida.* Manchester: Manchester University Press, 2005.

Dronsfield, Jonathan Lahey. "Filming Deconstruction/Deconstructing Film." *Love in the Post: From Plato to Derrida: The Screenplay and Commentary.* Ed. Joanna Callaghan and Martin McQuillan. London and New York: Rowman & Littlefield, 2014. 213–237.

Fargier, Jean-Paul, dir. *Mémoires d'aveugle: Le film de l'exposition.* 1990. VHS. Editions du Seuil/ Réunion des Musées Nationaux, 1992.

Fathy, Safaa. "Note d'intention." Jacques Derrida Archives 1949–2004. L'Institut Mémoires de l'édition contemporaine, Basse-Normandie, France.

———, dir. *D'Ailleurs, Derrida.* 2000. DVD. Éditions Montparnasse, 2008.

Gleiberman, Owen. Rev. of *Derrida*, dir. Kirby Dick and Amy Ziering Kofman. *Entertainment Weekly.* 15 November 2002. http://www.ew.com/article/2002/11/15/derrida.

Groen, Rick. "The Thinking Man's Film." Rev. of *Derrida*, dir. Kirby Dick and Amy Ziering Kofman. *The Globe and Mail.* 14 March 2003.

Herzog, Werner, dir. *Grizzly Man.* 2005. DVD. Maple Pictures, 2005.

Jeong, Seung-Hoon, and Dudley Andrew. "Grizzly Ghost: Herzog, Bazin and the Cinematic Animal." *Screen* 49.1 (2008): 1–12.

Lilly, Reginald. Rev. of *D'Ailleurs, Derrida*, by Safaa Fathy. *The French Review* 77.2 (December 2003): 393–395.

Lippit, Akira Mizuta. *Cinema without Reflection: Jacques Derrida's Echopoiesis and Narcissism Adrift.* Minneapolis: University of Minnesota Press, 2016.

Marker, Chris, dir. *La jetée/Sans soleil.* 1983. DVD. The Criterion Collection, 2007.

McMullen, Ken, dir. *Ghost Dance.* 1983. DVD. Mediabox, 2006.

Michaud, Ginette. *Veilleuses: Autour de trois images de Jacques Derrida*. Québec: Éditions Nota bene, 2009.

Mulvey, Laura. "Visual Pleasure and Narrative Cinema." *Screen* 16.3 (1975): 6–18.

Naas, Michael. *The End of the World and Other Teachable Moments: Jacques Derrida's Final Seminar*. New York: Fordham University Press, 2015.

Peeters, Benoît. *Derrida: A Biography*. Trans. Andrew Brown. Cambridge, UK: Polity Press, 2013.

Simmons, Laurence. "Jacques Derrida's Ghostface." *Angelaki: Journal of the Theoretical Humanities* 16.1 (March 2011): 129–141.

Sterritt, David. Rev. of *Derrida*, dir. Kirby Dick and Amy Ziering Kofman. *The Christian Science Monitor*. 25 October 2002. http://www.csmonitor.com/2002/1025/p12s01-almo.html.

Strathausen, Carsten. "The Philosopher's Body: Derrida and Teletechnology." *CR: The New Centennial Review* 9.2 (2009): 139–164.

Waugh, Thomas. *The Right to Play Oneself*. Minneapolis: University of Minnesota Press, 2011.

Conclusion: Spectral Glut

The word "ghost" is replete in histories of communication and archaeologies of media technology. It can be found in John Durham Peters and Friedrich Kittler; the latter of course being responsible for a turn away from media content and toward the technological aspects of media, the materialism of communicative events. Yet, media theorists have used this most troubling word and concept in their studies, rarely unpacking just what it is they mean by the kinds of ghosts that are to be found in the media culture. Many new media studies have simply conjured the word away without a second's thought. Not knowing whether to make heads or tails of *spectrality*, they think we can fully explain our media use without a critical history of its content. Derrida simply offers one of the most complex and thorough efforts to explain the ghost in the machine. That it related so closely and importantly to his project of deconstruction requires future scholars of the spectral in any form to treat the subject carefully and with the upmost seriousness. I also hoped to argue that its psychoanalytic definition is only an initial step that doesn't on its own relate the spectre to Derrida's ethico-political engagement.

In the age of information technology, how does spectrality work? "The one thing that one cannot accept these days—on television, on the radio, or in the papers—is an intellectual taking his time, or wasting other people's time," Derrida has said, noting the increased rhythm of mediatized speech and discourse (*Negotiations* 89). What would he have made of social media, like Twitter and

Facebook one wonders? His point about email in *Archive Fever* applies to the internet in general:

> [Email] is not only a technique, in the ordinary and limited sense of the term: at an unprecedented rhythm, in quasi-instantaneous fashion, this instrumental possibility of production, of printing, of conservation, and of destruction of the archive must inevitably be accompanied by juridical and thus political transformations. (17)

The speed of communication technology transforms the way the archive comes to be and how knowledge is produced. Spectral hauntings are working fast and furious in the information age. David Wills reminds us of the set-back of the intensification of speed and our modern mnemotechnologies: "[S]peed must threaten what I'll call, for rapidity's sake, the undecidability on which deconstruction also depends, not just the deliberateness that characterizes philosophical debate, but its whole interrogation of time-space" (*Matchbook* 103). In his final interview, Derrida made poignant observations on the nature of technological transformation and its relation to his own archive: "But today, the acceleration in the forms of archivization, though also use and destruction, are transforming the structure, temporality, and duration of the legacy" (*Learning* 33). He even went so far as to hypothesize that in the two weeks following his death there would be nothing left of his legacy. New methods of archiving will eclipse those of the past and therefore pose challenges to deconstruction as practised by him.

Social media today is designed for instantaneous information. We are encouraged to read only the newest responses and commentary and quickly respond in turn. The archive is in constant flux. But it is when we think we are responding spontaneously and off-the-cuff that we tend to rehearse the oldest ideas:

> Supposing, *concesso non dato*, that a living being ever responds in an absolutely living and infinitely well-adjusted manner, without the least automatism, without ever having an archival technique overflow the singularity of an event, we know in any case that a spectral response (thus informed by a *techne* and inscribed in an archive) is always possible. There would be neither history nor tradition nor culture without that possibility. (*Archive* 62–63)

What is the Internet but a veritable battleground of spectres? Images are more spectral than possibly ever. It's the element of unprogrammability and genuine surprise of the revenant of today's media traces that have to with its relation to justice. While much of the content on newsfeed repeats long-lasting mythic language and ideas, dominant spectres, once in a while on social media or elsewhere, we encounter citizen journalism that bears witness to policemen abusing their power or the plight of refugees from across the globe. The image of a dead Alan Kurdi arrests us with its emotional punch, but also speaks of the unprogrammability of social media.

Around the same time that Derrida's philosophy began to turn its attention toward more obviously ethical matters, and after the rise of the New Philosophers, it seems the visual or questions surrounding the visible also became important. It was only after the Prague incident and *Ghost Dance* that Derrida developed at length the concept of spectrality. What changed? The image is associated perhaps most with teletechnology operating at a global scale. Derrida's turn toward ethics very much went into these issues of global politics evinced perhaps most clearly by *Specters of Marx* and his work on hospitality. It seems fitting that the Other would now have to be thought in a globalized world. Regarding our consumption of information today, spectrality can shed light on what makes the powers of the media *both* space- and time-biased. As Naas points out in *Miracle and Machine*, televangelism offers a phantomatic transparency in the form of the voice (of God). Space-biased media of all kinds try to cover up their dependence on repetition. Prompted to explain the connection between the terms artifactuality and virtuality, Derrida states,

> I would insist not only on the *artificial* synthesis (synthetic image, synthetic voice, all the prosthetic supplements that can take the place of the real actuality) but also on the concept of *virtuality* (virtual image, virtual space, and thus virtual event), which certainly can no longer be opposed with philosophical equanimity to actual reality … Today a philosopher who "thinks his time" must, among other things, be attentive to the implications and consequences of this virtual time—both to the novelties of its technical uses, but also to what in what is new recalls possibilities much more ancient. (*Negotiations* 89)

The question of belief in the hauntological era cannot be underplayed. On 9/11, Derrida has said the repetition of the footage of the planes crashing into the Twin Towers ensured an endless violence, fuelling anger throughout the globe. With 9/11, Bazin's "dying every afternoon" was expanded to "disaster every minute" on an eternal loop. Media compulsively replayed the footage trying to analyze it in every possible way. The event wasn't adequately understood, best exemplified by the unspecific name "9/11" itself. The event, Derrida argues,

> remains ineffable, like an intuition without a concept, like a unicity with no generality on the horizon or with no horizon at all, out of range for a language that admits its powerlessness and so is reduced to pronouncing mechanically a date, repeating it endlessly, as a kind of ritual incantation, a conjuring poem, a journalistic litany or rhetorical refrain that admits to not knowing what it's talking about. (Borradori 86)

Media that tap into religious belief are especially relevant for future studies. Al-Qaeda and more recently ISIL (Islamic State of Iraq and the Levant) videos circulate the interwebs and are further disseminated by mainstream news media and even democratic governments, like in Canada's 42nd general election campaign (Daro). Possibly the most dangerous spectral media of the 21st century, these videos blend religion and violence in ways that makes them both clandestine and seemingly just for their intended audience.

Aren't all spectral images somewhat about exclusion? The contemporary mass migration crisis has garnered unprecedented attention from photojournalists. Many of the images coming out of it are deeply intelligent and truly haunting. Images of refugees in camps, waiting at borders, or walking through the mud confer dignity onto their subjects. But the ISIL videos also haunt. The refugee photo wants to recruit those that respect the other while the ISIL image recruits those that hate and want to inflict harm. One is about exclusion while the other wants to exclude. Both types of images want to recruit—they are calls for help.

One important and problematic limitation to these theoretical pursuits is that Derrida never had anything relevant to say about glut or information overload. There is a sense with Derrida ethics is coextensive with revealing the technological nature of our world, the way machines trade absence for presence; the dead for what is alive. Are we so far off today from the celebrations of the victory of neo-liberalism that marked period of the late 1980s? How does society today seek to eradicate all ghosts in favour of the presentism of social media? Derrida expressed the importance of engaging with the ghost of Marx. He understood the part teletechnology (his word for mass communication, television, telephone, internet) plays in compelling us to ignore the past. At the same time, teletechnology could also provide answers to this logocentrism and could critique neo-liberalism through its inherent and autoimmune spectral powers and radical critique. There are indications in *Specters of Marx* that Derrida sees the ways we communicate with each other as key to political engagement. The abstract structure of spectrality is developed at length at this point. If the ghost of *Specters* is too abstract, in *Echographies* we get a more concrete application of the idea with references to *Ghost Dance*, a film that conjures as many ghosts as it possibly can, including those of Ogier, Derrida himself, the communards, ancient civilizations, city dwellers, Freud, Marx, and Kafka. In *Echographies*, the experience of being photographed itself is seen as spectral. The one who is performing is both ghost and watched by the ghost. So, as we proceed today and in the future let's be the kinds of ghosts that we can all get behind.

Bibliography

Borradori, Giovanna. *Philosophy in a Time of Terror: Dialogues with Jürgen Habermas and Jacques Derrida*. Chicago, IL: University of Chicago Press, 2003.

Daro, Ishmael N. "Conservative ad Uses ISIL Propaganda and Anthem to Attack Trudeau's Foreign Policy." *National Post* (25 June 2015). Web. 9 February 2016.

Derrida, Jacques. *Archive Fever: A Freudian Impression*. Trans. Eric Prenowitz. Chicago, IL: University of Chicago Press, 1996.

———. *Negotiations: Interventions and Interviews 1971–2001*. Ed. and Trans. Elizabeth Rottenberg. Stanford, CA: Stanford University Press, 2002.

———. *Learning to Live Finally: The Last Interview*. Trans. Pascale-Anne Brault and Michael Naas. Hoboken, NJ: Melville House Publishing, 2007.

Wills, David. *Matchbook: Essays in Deconstruction*. Stanford, CA: Stanford University Press, 2005.

Index

.

Lightning Source UK Ltd.
Milton Keynes UK
UKHW020919191220
375442UK00003B/195